TRANSFORMED
LIVING

TRANSFORMED
LIVING

Living **out** your life
Ephesians 4–6

DAVE SMITH

CWR

Christians are called to more than superficial change. God invites us to nothing less than profound, supernatural transformation. This practical, inspirational book, coming from the heart and mind of Dave Smith, one of the UK's most dynamic and anointed Christian leaders, points the way.

– Jeff Lucas, author, speaker, broadcaster

Dave Smith is one of the most inspirational Christian leaders in the UK today. I am delighted to recommend this, his second book of reflections on Ephesians. His teaching provides profound insights, helping us to grow in service to Jesus Christ.

– Nicky Gumbel, Vicar of HTB

I'm delighted to commend this second volume of devotions by my friend Dave Smith on Paul's letter to the Ephesians. This book has many merits, not least wisdom, balance and insight, but above all it lets the mind-stretching and faith-expanding message of Ephesians speak to us today!

– J.John, author, speaker, minister

Having established our new identity in Ephesians 1–3, let's move on to discover our responsibilities to live worthy of such a calling and, filled with the Holy Spirit, humbly find our place in the body of Christ and stand strong, fully armed for the battle. Dave is well qualified to help you on the journey.

– Terry Virgo, Founder of Newfrontiers

Often daily devotionals, though helpful, don't offer systematic study or biblical depth – they tend to highlight a thought for the day with a short application idea. How refreshing to be able to study the Scriptures for 50 days with continuity, content and contemporary application!

– Stuart Bell, Senior Pastor of Alive Church and Leader of the Ground Level Network

There are two reasons why you should read this book. First, my friend Dave is a doctor; he must have something profound to say! Second, he chooses what I consider to be one of the most exciting books of the Bible and details an issue we all struggle with. The book of Ephesians addresses the place of the Christian in society today. Do we find our identity in our past challenges, present dilemmas or future uncertainties? Do we find our identity in purpose alone or our standing in Christ? Once our identity is clear, the second challenge we ask is, 'How to live worthy of our calling?' If you like answers to life's questions, this is the book you need to read!

– Glyn Barrett, Senior Minister of !Audacious Church, UK

CONTENTS

INTRODUCTION

Welcome to *Transformed Living*, a devotional based on Ephesians 4–6. I am so excited for what the Lord is going to do in you as you go on this 50-day spiritual journey.

Ephesians is a marvellous letter, variously described as 'the crown of Paul's writings'[1] and (apart from Romans), a letter that is considered to have had 'the most influence on Christian thought and spirituality'.[2] It seems likely that Ephesians was a circular to Christians in the whole region of Asia Minor, of which Ephesus was the centre. Contained within this short letter are some of the most comprehensive and marvellous descriptions of what it means to be transformed, and to live a transformed life in and through a relationship with Jesus Christ. The previous book, *Transformed Life*, was based on Ephesians 1–3 and focused on finding biblical answers to three of life's great questions: Who am I? Where do I belong? What am I living for? The answers are found by looking at what God the Father has done for us in Christ and by the Spirit, and by seeing that we now have a glorious new identity, place of belonging and purpose in Christ. *Transformed Living* builds on this foundation by looking at Ephesians 4–6, where the focus switches to us living in the light of what Christ has done for us and of who we have now become in Him. In the words of John Stott: 'Now the apostle … turns from exposition to exhortation … from doctrine to duty … from mind-stretching theology to its down-to-earth, concrete implications in everyday living'.[3]

In Ephesians 4–6 there is a particular focus on the unity and purity of the people of God, and of how being in Christ shapes our relationships in the home and the workplace, helping us to prevail in spiritual warfare. This study is divided up into seven weeks with specific emphases:

- Week 1 (4:1–6) – walking worthy of our calling in Christ, with a particular focus on keeping the unity of the Spirit.
- Week 2 (4:7–16) – recognising and utilising the unique gifts that each of us have been given as essential for the growth in unity and maturity of the whole body of Christ.
- Week 3 (4:17–32) – no longer living according to our old life, but living the new life in Christ, in the very practical areas of our attitudes, speech and lifestyle.
- Week 4 (5:1–14) – living in love and light, and choosing to shun the darkness.
- Week 5 (5:15–21) – walking in wisdom and being filled with the Spirit.
- Week 6 (5:22–6:9) – honouring Christ by the way we honour each other in the home and workplace.
- Week 7 (6:10–20) – standing strong in the Lord, putting on the full armour of God and prevailing against evil.
- Day 50 (6:21–24) – celebrating our relationships with each other and with our triune God.

How to get the best from this devotional guide

The purpose of this devotional guide is to help us digest these wonderful truths in bite-sized chunks. So, every day for the next 50 days, we are going to be studying a verse or verses from Ephesians 4–6, which will help paint a picture of transformed living. In order to benefit the most, it is important to invest the appropriate time. So, as well as setting aside a few minutes each day to read each section, it is important to follow this up with personal reflection and response. A recent survey[4] of how people grow in their spiritual journey with Christ highlighted that the number one spiritual growth tool (twice as influential as any other practice) was the discipline of regularly reading and reflecting on Scripture. If you are already in this discipline then hopefully this study will give you some extra material to use alongside your daily devotions.

For others, my hope and prayer is that this will set you on a course of daily reading and reflecting on Scripture that will last a lifetime! In addition to this personal devotional, which I trust will be of great blessing to many, maximum benefit will be gained when this is studied along with others in the context of the community of the local church. So we have produced the following free materials for churches and small groups to use:

- Sermon outlines
- Small group videos
- Small group studies

To get started, may I encourage you to set aside a time this week to read through the whole of the letter to the Ephesians in one sitting. Get yourself a drink and find somewhere quiet, then read a modern version of the Bible either via an app, online or a paper version. We are using the New International Version (2011, Anglicised) for this study, so it might help if you do the same. Then slowly and out loud read through all six chapters. When you have finished, pray!

TRANSFORMED
LIVING

This 50-day devotional underpins the 7-week church programme, Transformed Living. Explore, together with your church, how to live out the Christian life through Ephesians 4–6.

How to get your church involved

1. Sign up online to access free resources
2. Invite your church to take part
3. Order your 50-day devotionals (bulk discounts available)

Free resources for your leaders

• Sermon outlines
• Small group videos
• Small group studies

www.transformed-living.info

TRANSFORMED (LIFE)

Find out more about Transformed Life at the back of this book or visit **www.transformed-life.info**

WEEK 1
LIVING WORTHY, KEEPING UNITY

'As a prisoner for the Lord, then, I urge you to live a life worthy of the calling you have received. Be completely humble and gentle; be patient, bearing with one another in love. Make every effort to keep the unity of the Spirit through the bond of peace. There is one body and one Spirit, just as you were called to one hope when you were called; one Lord, one faith, one baptism; one God and Father of all, who is over all and through all and in all.'

EPHESIANS 4:1–6

NEW IDENTITY, NEW LIFE

'I therefore, a prisoner for the Lord, urge you to walk in a manner worthy of the calling to which you have been called' **EPHESIANS 4:1 (ESV)**

One of my favourite films is *Les Misérables*. Set in early nineteenth-century France, it focuses on Jean Valjean, a French peasant who has spent 19 years in prison for stealing a loaf of bread for his sister's starving child. One day, Valjean decides to break parole, is caught stealing again, is pardoned by an extraordinary act of mercy and generosity from a kindly bishop, and commissioned to live a transformed life in the service of God and others. In the novel by Victor Hugo, which the film is based on, the bishop declares these powerful words: 'Jean Valjean, my brother, you no longer belong to evil, but to good. It is your soul that I buy from you; I withdraw it from black thoughts and the spirit of perdition, and I give it to God.'[1] Overwhelmed by this act of grace and embracing his new identity, Valjean goes out and lives a radical life of love, kindness and generosity, transforming the lives of others, before dying a free and fulfilled man.

In many ways, Valjean's story is a great depiction of the Christian life, a picture that we see more fully and gloriously portrayed in Paul's marvellous letter to the Ephesians: our lives have been transformed by extraordinary grace, we have received a new identity in Christ, and now we are called to live the rest of our lives in the service of God and others. Paul begins the second half of his letter, here in Ephesians 4:1, like the bishop, commissioning us to live differently in the light of what we have received and who we have now become: 'I therefore, a prisoner for the Lord, urge you to walk in a manner worthy of the calling to which you have been called' (Eph. 4:1, ESV).

Notice, first, Paul's use of the hugely important word 'therefore' ('then' in the NIV). It points back to what God has done for us in Christ, as the basis for how we must now live lives 'worthy of the calling' to which we 'have been called'. This calling Paul has already laid out in great detail in Ephesians 1–3 (the focus of our previous study, *Transformed Life*). At the heart of our calling is the fact that like Valjean, but in a far greater way, our lives have been transformed by grace. This grace is shown in the fact that before the creation of the world, God the Father chose us in Christ, predestined us to be adopted as His children and then through Christ's coming, redeemed, forgave and sealed us with His Spirit, thus guaranteeing our full inheritance in the ages to come (see 1:3–14). This great calling involves us being freed from spiritual slavery, being spiritually raised from the dead, being made alive with Christ and seated with Him in heavenly places (2:1–6). Now we have a transformed identity as God's workmanship, His new creation. We also have a new life purpose, which is to carry out the good works that He has planned in advance for us to do (2:10). Finally, we have a new place of belonging, as members of His family, as citizens of His kingdom, and as a part of His new temple (2:19–22).

Like Valjean, now that we are recipients of such grace and have received this glorious new identity, place of belonging and purpose, we 'therefore' can and must live the rest of our lives according to this new agenda, in a manner worthy of this great calling. The order is important: before we focus on what we must do, we need to pause and remind ourselves what He has done! A painting illustration that I heard many years ago may help. I remember as a young school child in art class being instructed to start my pictures by covering the paper with a blue wash. Before I went to the brown for the tree trunk and the green for the leaves, it was vital that I let the blue wash dry, or my painting would be a confusing mess! It's the same for us as Christians. We must let the revelation of grace, of what God has done for us in Christ and who we now are in Him, really settle in our hearts and minds before rushing out to try and live that new life. Hence the importance of properly pausing and taking time to work through the following reflect and respond section.

REFLECT AND RESPOND

- Before we set out on this journey over the next 50 days, take some time before tomorrow to read or reread Ephesians 1–3 (preferably out loud). If you have read *Transformed Life*, you may want to revisit any key studies that particularly spoke to you.

- If you are a Christian, take time to praise God for the huge privilege of being 'in Christ'.

- If you are not a Christian, I'm so glad you have decided to read this! Ask God to reveal Himself to you as you go on this journey over the next 50 days.

MEMORY VERSE

'Make every effort to keep the unity of the Spirit through the bond of peace.'
EPHESIANS 4:3

LIVE LIKE ROYALTY

'I therefore, a prisoner for the Lord, urge you to walk in a manner worthy of the calling to which you have been called' **EPHESIANS 4:1 (ESV)**

What immediately springs to mind when you hear the phrase 'living like royalty'? Do you think of the *privileges* or the *responsibilities* associated with high office? Throughout history and in our world today, sadly we have seen many examples of people abusing the privileges and neglecting the responsibilities of their position. What a great contrast Queen Elizabeth II has been! Born third in line to the British throne, she suddenly became heiress in 1936, when her uncle Edward first became king and then abdicated, leaving her father, 'the stuttering Duke of York', to succeed as King George VI. Many years later, on her 21st birthday in 1947, she promised to her people in famous words: 'my whole life, whether it be long or short, shall be devoted to your service'.[1] Since she was crowned and anointed as Queen Elizabeth II in 1953, she has retained this acute awareness of the huge sense of responsibility, borne out of a deep awareness of her high calling and privilege.

In Ephesians 4:1 Paul says something similar, but even greater, applying it to all Christians. In chapters 1–3, he has already laid out the privileges of what it means to be in Christ, sons and daughters of the living God, seated with Christ the King as princes and princesses in the royal heavenly family! Now he moves on in chapters 4–6 to lay out the responsibilities of that high calling: 'I therefore, a prisoner for the Lord, urge you to walk in a manner worthy of the calling to which you have been called' (4:1, ESV).

Paul starts by referring to his own calling. He is no longer Saul, persecutor of the Church, imprisoning and killing Christians. Now he has a glorious new identity as Paul a 'prisoner for the Lord' – literally a prisoner *in* the Lord, devoted to or captive to Christ. Thus, he serves as a personal example of a gloriously transformed life. He is carrying out this new responsibility to the utmost, since he is also literally in prison for the sake of Christ, having given his life for the gospel. Hence he has authority as Christ's apostle – or 'sent one' – to bring Christ's message to the Ephesians then and to us today.

It is also significant how he addresses Jesus here as 'Lord' rather than 'Christ', which was his favourite term in Ephesians 1–3. In fact, of the 26 references to Jesus as 'Lord' in this letter, 20 are found in chapters 4–6. The term 'Lord' (*Kurios* in Greek, or *Adonai* in Hebrew), is what the Jews called God due to an avoidance of using God's name 'Yahweh' during that era. The use of the term 'Lord' here serves to emphasise that we have moved from focusing on rejoicing in our salvation 'in Christ' to living our lives 'worthy' of the one who is 'Lord' and therefore is Yahweh – God.

Having focused on his own example, and reminding the Ephesians, and us, of his authority to speak on behalf of the Lord, he now gets to the seriousness of his challenge, encapsulated in the phrase 'I urge you'. Years ago, when I was a new Christian, I occasionally heard people say, 'Just let go, and let God!' Paul would rather say, '*I urge you* to live a life worthy of the calling you have received.'

The literal translation of the word 'live' (NIV), is 'walk' (ESV), which carries the sense of a focused determination to keep moving forward in a particular direction. This highlights that becoming a Christian is not a short-term, half-hearted decision, but rather a permanent change of life and lifestyle. This call to transformed living is a call to live in a way that is 'worthy', fitting or becoming of who we have now become in Christ, to truly 'live like royalty'. In the rest of Ephesians 4–6 Paul more fully unpacks what living this new life looks like: a life of unity (4:2–6), diversity (4:7–16), purity (4:16–5:21), harmony (5:22–6:9), and victory (6:10–20). This week we will focus on 4:1–6 and on the call to unity.

REFLECT AND RESPOND

- **Thank God for the privilege of being His son or daughter, a member of His heavenly royal family! Think about this amazing truth.**

- **Ask the Lord to forgive you for where you have perhaps fallen short of this high calling and responsibility.**

- **Invite Him to speak to you during these studies and empower you to start living a life 'worthy' of the call.**

MEMORY VERSE

'Make every effort to keep the unity of the Spirit through the bond of peace.'
EPHESIANS 4:3

CHRISTLIKE CHARACTER

'Be completely humble and gentle; be patient, bearing with one another in love.' **EPHESIANS 4:2**

In his highly influential book, *Good to Great*, researcher and author Jim Collins analyses the reasons why some companies were able to go from good to great whereas similar companies in the same field failed to do so. First on the list of factors was that the 'great' companies were led by 'Level 5' leaders, people who displayed a high degree of 'personal humility', and whose focused ambition and determination was 'first and foremost for the institution and not for themselves'.[1] Similarly and unsurprisingly, in a follow-up book, *How the Mighty Fall*, Collins concludes that the first factor as to why organisations begin to decline is 'hubris', which is the opposite of humility but rather an 'excessive pride that brings down a hero'.[2]

Two thousand years earlier the apostle Paul makes a similar point. His concern in his letter to the Ephesians is the health, unity and success of the greatest organisation on planet Earth, the Church of Jesus Christ. Hence, before addressing the priority of unity (4:3–6), he focuses in on a list of character qualities that all believers are to display. Significantly, first on his list is 'humility'.

Humility was a word that was rarely used in Greek literature of the day, but almost always in a derogatory way. It literally meant 'lowliness of mind' and is a foundational virtue in Christianity, as modelled by Christ Himself. Christ's deliberate self-humbling and God-exaltation (Phil. 2:1–9) sets a whole new example for His followers. This humility is, as C.S. Lewis points out, 'not thinking less of yourself; it is thinking of yourself less'.[3] This frees us to think about others and their needs, and is a key foundation for living in unity.

The second characteristic, 'gentleness', is linked to this emphasis on humility. Sometimes misleadingly translated as 'meekness', which implies weakness, true gentleness is a quality of the strong, who exercise their strength under control. The gentle use their strength for the benefit of others – another truly vital characteristic for unity.

The next two qualities, 'patience' and 'bearing with one another' (forbearance), are linked, since we need to practise both if we are to live with others in harmony. The simple fact of the matter is that none of us have arrived or are perfect, and therefore we must be prepared to make allowances for each other's imperfections. I know I still have many faults, which my wife Karen is generally very patient about. There is one exception: I regularly go out of the house with my trousers tucked into my socks. That really tests her patience. I can't understand why! Of course, in many situations and relationships we can spot much more serious deficiencies in others (and they in us), so we need together to allow the Spirit to help us exercise patience and forbearance.

If Paul led out with the importance of humility, he fittingly concludes this list with 'love'. This love is not the human kind of love that can fluctuate with emotions, but is *agape* love, the unconditional, giving type of love that ultimately comes from God Himself. Paul has already celebrated how this 'great love' caused the Father to rescue us from our spiritual death and make us alive in Christ (2:4–5). He has also prayed that we might be 'rooted and established' in this love, and that 'together with all the Lord's holy people we might 'grasp how wide and long and high and deep is the love of Christ' (3:17–18). Here in 4:2, the apostle is emphasising that it is this same love with which we are to love 'one another'.

These character qualities of humility, gentleness, patience, forbearance and love, come from Christ and are essential if we are to keep the unity of the Spirit, which is the focal point for the rest of this week's studies.

REFLECT AND RESPOND

- Take a few moments today to look back over the list of five character qualities. Which of them do you think you need to grow in the most?

- Ask God to show you any unhelpful attitudes you may be harbouring at the moment. Invite Him to fill you with His Holy Spirit to empower you to become more like Christ in these areas so that you can become a catalyst for unity, not discord.

MEMORY VERSE

'Make every effort to keep the unity of the Spirit through the bond of peace.'

EPHESIANS 4:3

KEEP THE UNITY
OF THE SPIRIT

'Make every effort to keep the unity of the Spirit
through the bond of peace.' **EPHESIANS 4:3**

One of the most popular British TV programmes of the last 20 years was
called *Ground Force*. In each episode, a team of gardeners would give a
complete makeover to the garden of a nominated individual. With the
individual away, the team would work to transform the garden over
two days, much to the delighted surprise of the person on their return.
And that's where the programme would finish. For the new garden,
however, that was not the end but just the beginning. In order for it to
retain its beauty and order, it would need the hard work of continual
watering, feeding and weeding!

Here Paul is saying something similar. He is referring to the great
corporate 'makeover' that we as Christians have received, having
been freed from our alienation from God and from one another,
and having been brought together in the glorious harmony and
unity of one people in Christ (see Eph. 2:11–22). But that's not the
end of the matter. God has done His part in creating this unity.
Now our job is to 'make every effort to keep the unity of the Spirit
in the bond of peace'. In other words, we have to maintain what
God has already done.

First, notice the priority of unity. Of all the emphases that Paul
could have picked up on, his primary concern for those who have

been transformed by Christ, is the call to continue to live together as a united body and a harmonious family. For those of us who live in the individualistic Western world, it's important for us to grasp that God's primary concern is for us to live out our new life in the context of a united community, the Church.

Second, it is important to note the urgency of this call. The phrase 'make every effort' means that we are to be continuous and diligent in the pursuit of keeping this unity. As one commentator puts it: 'It is hardly possible to render exactly the urgency contained in the underlying Greek verb. Not only haste and passion, but a full effort of the whole man is meant, involving his will, sentiment, reason, physical strength and total attitude. The imperative mood … excludes passivity, quietism, a wait-and-see attitude or a diligence tempered by all deliberate speed. Yours is the initiative! Do it now! Mean it! *You* are to do it! I mean it!'[1]

Third, this unity that we are to keep is 'in the bond of peace'. The word peace used here and elsewhere in Paul's writings refers most frequently not to inner peace (as in Phil. 4:7), but to relational peace between people. In this context it is talking about making every effort to keep the unity of the Spirit by living at peace, or we might say, 'in harmony' with other Christians.

What does this look like in practice? Bear in mind that as Paul was writing to the Ephesians he was writing most likely to a group of churches in and around Ephesus. Hence we need to seek to live this out, first within the local church. This is where *every* believer needs to belong and to live out and work out his or her calling. We also need to seek to live this out within the context of the broader Church – with other congregations of different expressions and affiliation.

How are we to do this? Rick Warren, in *The Purpose Driven Life*,[2] gives us a few very helpful practical instructions:

- Focus on what we have in common, not our differences
- Be realistic in our expectations
- Choose to encourage rather than criticise

- Refuse to listen to gossip
- Practise God's method for conflict resolution (see Matt.18:15–17)
- Support your pastor and leaders.

REFLECT AND RESPOND

- **As you reflect and respond, think how you can be a greater catalyst for unity, starting within your church.**

- **Can you think of any ways, either in your thoughts, attitudes or actions, where you recognise you haven't made *every* effort to maintain unity, either within your church or among other groups?**

- **What steps can you take to rectify this?**

MEMORY VERSE

'Make every effort to keep the unity of the Spirit through the bond of peace.'
EPHESIANS 4:3

UNITY BASED ON ONE BODY, ONE SPIRIT, ONE HOPE

'There is one body and one Spirit, just as you were called to one hope when you were called; one Lord, one faith, one baptism; one God and Father of all, who is over all and through all and in all.' **EPHESIANS 4:4–6**

I don't know what your main priorities are in life right now. Perhaps they are your job, your health, your finances, or your family. All of these are important and matter very much to God, but it's important that as His children we embrace the things that really matter to Him. Right near the top of God's priorities is the unity of His family.

We have seen this in the previous verse, how Paul urges us to make 'every effort to keep the unity of the Spirit' (4:3). Here in 4:4–6, he now grounds his appeal on the strongest possible foundation: the very unity of God Himself. He does this partly through the use of certain important biblical numbers: one, three and seven. The repetition of the number one is a deliberate reference to the unity of God Himself (see, for example, the *Shema*: 'Hear, O Israel ... the LORD is one' from Deut. 6:4). Then notice that our oneness is based on the God who is also three in one, with the 'one Spirit', the 'one Lord', and the 'one God and Father' all in very clear view. This highlights the awesomeness of our unity, which flows from the tri-unity of God. Finally, notice that there are seven 'ones'. Seven is often described as the language of perfection or divine completion (see Isa. 11), and serves here to emphasise the perfection of the unity that we have by God's grace. We will unpack these seven 'ones' over the next few days.

Today, we start where Paul starts: with an emphasis on our unity being based on the fact that 'there is *one body* and *one Spirit*, just as you were called to *one hope* when you were called' (4:4, my italics). First, Paul starts with an emphasis on the 'one body', because this most immediately relates to us. The human body is Paul's favourite image to describe the Church. In 1:22–23 he has painted a magnificent picture of how Jesus, the 'head', has been raised up and exalted over everything for the Church, 'which is his body, the fullness of him who fills everything in every way'. Then in 2:15–16 he goes on to emphasise that this body is made up of reconciled Jews and Gentiles. The fact that we are now 'members together of one body' highlights how close our unity is, and how important it is that we keep working together in harmony. If the members of our own physical bodies need to work in unison, how much more the members of Christ's spiritual body, the Church.

Second, Paul emphasises, as he has done already in 4:3, that we are one body because we have 'one Spirit'. It is through the 'one Spirit' that we have joint access to the Father (2:18). It is also through the same Spirit that the Father is present with us in Christ, since we are being made to be a dwelling 'in which God lives by his Spirit' (2:22). The fact that the same Spirit of God dwells in every Christian is what joins us together in Christ. In the light of this glory, how tragic it is that the Church is often the place of such disunity!

Thirdly, our unity is based on 'one hope', our shared hope as the people of God. Paul has earlier painted a glorious picture of our future eternal hope when God will 'bring unity to all things in heaven and on earth under Christ' (1:10). As one commentator emphasises: 'The one hope of Ephesians is not something individual and private but corporate and public, hope for a cosmos that is unified and reconciled, a world in which everything is brought together in harmony through that which God has done in Christ … The one hope of final cosmic unity is therefore meant to produce the urgent effort to maintain and demonstrate the anticipation of this in the Church.'[1]

The grounds for unity couldn't be stronger. Through the sovereign grace of God, all Christians everywhere (including Jews and Gentiles of every denomination and affiliation) have been united in one body. Through that same grace we have been filled with one Spirit, through whom we enjoy the present experience and the future promise that we will have a glorious future hope together.

REFLECT AND RESPOND

- **Meditate on God's nature as unity: three Persons in one. Pray that you would be able to represent the love of the Father, the grace of the Son, the encouragement of the Holy Spirit in the way you relate to others.**

- **Thank God for the privilege of being united with His people – in one body, by one Spirit, with one shared hope – and determine today to make every effort to respond to this privilege in your own relationships.**

MEMORY VERSE

'Make every effort to keep the unity of the Spirit through the bond of peace.'
EPHESIANS 4:3

UNITY BASED ON ONE LORD, ONE FAITH, ONE BAPTISM

'one Lord, one faith, one baptism' **EPHESIANS 4:5**

I have followed my football team, Manchester City, from the high days of the late sixties, through the 40 years in the wilderness, to the current days of favour! Much to my wife's dismay, this competitiveness often spills over into not wanting 'rival' teams to win. Whether you can identify more with me or my wife on this, when it comes to being a follower of Christ, we must agree to lay aside all competitiveness and rivalry and embrace the glorious fact that as Christians *we are all on the same side*. Paul puts it much more magnificently and succinctly: 'there is one Lord, one faith, one baptism'.

The 'Lord' here is a clear reference to Jesus Christ, the Son of God, joined with the Spirit (4:4) and the Father (4:6) in a glorious trinity. The term 'Lord' was the title for Yahweh in the Old Testament (see Day 2; fn. O'Brien, *Ephesians*, p283). Through his encounter with Jesus on the road to Damascus, Paul came to recognise that Jesus was in fact 'Lord' (Acts 9:5–6). This revelation clearly shapes Paul's theology in Ephesians, where he frequently links the Father and Jesus together (see 1:2,3,15,17) and sometimes with the Spirit, too (2:18,21–22; 3:14–19). In terms of the call to unity, there could not be a clearer motivation: we have 'one Lord', who is Jesus Christ. There is one head of the Church, Jesus Christ (1:21–22), and in and through this one Lord we have been blessed, chosen, predestined, redeemed, forgiven and sealed, and in and through Him we will all eternally be one. Since there is only one head, it is imperative that we live in unity and harmony with the other members of His body.

On the foundation of knowing that there is 'one Lord' Paul moves on to emphasise that we have 'one faith'. The use of the term 'faith' here most likely refers to the objective set of beliefs that are at the very heart of true Christianity, which centres on the person and work of Christ. This serves to highlight that our unity must be based on the truth of the gospel. However, there is a big difference between standing for core beliefs and splitting over minor and often trivial distinctions. I heard a story of two congregations located only a few blocks from each other in a small community that had decided to unite as one larger and more effective body, instead of being two struggling churches. But the merger did not happen because they could not agree on how to recite the Lord's Prayer. One group wanted 'forgive us our trespasses', while the other demanded 'forgive us our debts'! The point is not that they necessarily should have merged, but that they shouldn't have remained separate over such a trivial matter.

From 'one Lord' and 'one faith', Paul proceeds to 'one baptism'. It seems most likely that the baptism here is water baptism. Sadly, this has been one of the most divisive issues in church history. In its New Testament context, baptism was a way of publicly declaring one's faith and identifying with the people of God, sometimes at great cost. It is the same in parts of our world today. A few years ago I heard of a country where Christians were being persecuted for their faith. If someone was found to have converted to Christ, they were put in prison for one year. If they were found to have been baptised, they were put in prison for five years. There is something about having been baptised that indicates a full-on, public declaration of discipleship. In effect it means, in the words of one author: 'Count me in. I mean business.'[1] This 'one baptism' is meant to be one of the foundations of our unity.

REFLECT AND RESPOND

- Take a few moments to read out loud this phrase: 'one Lord, one faith, one baptism'. Meditate on the truth that there is only one Lord, Jesus Christ, who is head of the whole Church.

- Allow this truth to deeply impact your attitudes and actions towards other Christians – both within your church and in the universal Church.

- What changes do you need to make as a result?

MEMORY VERSE

'Make every effort to keep the unity of the Spirit through the bond of peace.'

EPHESIANS 4:3

UNITY BASED ON ONE GOD AND FATHER

'one God and Father of all, who is over all and through all and in all.' **EPHESIANS 4:6**

I remember there was a season when our two daughters were much younger, that they seemed to be incessantly squabbling. Invariably the issues were pretty trivial – like the younger one 'borrowing' the older one's hair bobbles – which caused us as parents some concern! Thankfully, as they grew up they became much more gracious towards one another, and remain very good friends to this day – something that brings joy to us as their mum and dad.

Similarly, there must be something about us not getting along as God's children that causes grief to our heavenly Father, and us living in harmony that gives Him great joy. Paul, having begun with our practical experience as Christians – united in one body, filled with *one Spirit*, who is a guarantee of our one hope – moves on to the centrality of us being under *one Lord*, sharing one faith and baptism, and finishes with the acknowledgement that there is 'one God and Father of all, who is over all and through all and in all'. Once again, the basis for unity couldn't be stronger since we *all* have the same God and Father.

So, who are the 'all' referred to four times in this single verse (4:6)? It could refer to *all Christians*, especially given that the emphasis in this passage is on the unity of God's people, and elsewhere the Father is referred to as the 'God and Father of our Lord Jesus Christ' and therefore 'our' Father (eg 1:2, 1:3–6; 1:17; 2:18). Certainly, the fact that all Christians have one God and Father, and therefore are part of the same family, is a huge incentive to keeping the unity of the Spirit.

However, it seems more likely that while the 'all' definitely includes all Christians, it is intended to encompass something even broader: the whole of Creation. In 1:9–10, we can see that God's ultimate goal is the reuniting of the whole cosmos under one head, Christ, of which the unity of the Church (2:11–22) is at the centre. In the words of one commentator: 'The unity of the church is the means by which the manifold wisdom of God is being displayed to the universe. The church is … the pilot project of God's purposes and his people are the expression of this unity that displays to the universe his final goal'.[1]

If this is the case, and in the light of obvious divisions today, how can we respond? It is important to point out that there is a difference between the invisible unity that exists in Christ and the visible unity that needs working on! But this doesn't mean we shouldn't work on it. In fact, Paul's whole point is that we are one in the Spirit (invisibly), and therefore we should give great effort to living this unity out, visibly.

As we finish this week's study let me conclude with a quote from the great nineteenth-century preacher, Charles Spurgeon: 'If there were two lords, you might be divided into two parties; if there were two faiths, you might split up into two sections; if there were two baptisms, you might be right in having two denominations; if there were two fathers, there might be two families; if there were two indwelling spirits, there would be, and there must be, two sorts of people; but, in the true Church of Jesus Christ, there is "one God and Father of all, who is above all, and through all, and in you all."'[2] Since this is the case we must endeavour to maintain this unity as an utmost priority.

REFLECT AND RESPOND

- **Pray for the unity of your church. Ask the Lord to help you become someone who promotes and maintains unity within your church family.**

- **Determine to be someone who, in your words, actions and prayers, honours other Christians and churches, regardless of their denomination.**

MEMORY VERSE

'Make every effort to keep the unity of the Spirit through the bond of peace.'

EPHESIANS 4:3

WEEK 2
UNITY AND MATURITY THROUGH DIVERSITY

'But to each one of us grace has been given as Christ apportioned it. This is why it says: "When he ascended on high, he took many captives and gave gifts to his people."
(What does "he ascended" mean except that he also descended to the lower, earthly regions? He who descended is the very one who ascended higher than all the heavens, in order to fill the whole universe.) So Christ himself gave the apostles, the prophets, the evangelists, the pastors and teachers, to equip his people for works of service, so that the body of Christ may be built up until we all reach unity in the faith and in the knowledge of the Son of God and become mature, attaining to the whole measure of the fullness of Christ.
Then we will no longer be infants, tossed back and forth by the waves, and blown here and there by every wind of teaching and by the cunning and craftiness of people in their deceitful scheming. Instead, speaking the truth in love, we will grow to become in every respect the mature body of him who is the head, that is, Christ. From him the whole body, joined and held together by every supporting ligament, grows and builds itself up in love, as each part does its work.'

EPHESIANS 4:7–16

DAY 8

YOU HAVE A GIFT!

'But to each one of us grace has been given as Christ apportioned it.' **EPHESIANS 4:7**

It's not my favourite sport, but there is one aspect of Formula 1 that even I find amazing: that is the individual skills and teamwork that contribute towards the ultimate goal of winning. You will sometimes see a driver limp into the pit lane with a puncture and the front wing of his car hanging off, only to be back out racing within a matter of seconds. This 'miracle' is of course the result of an incredibly well-trained and well-prepared team who know exactly what their individual jobs are as the car comes in for a pit stop. And what a sight it is... wheels are pulled off, new wheels seem to zoom in from nowhere, whole parts of cars are taken off and replaced, and all in the blink of an eye. Particularly impressive to someone such as me with my almost complete lack of engineering skills! The overall lesson, of course, is that in Formula 1 each member of the team has to play his or her part if they are to achieve the big goal of winning the race.

Paul is making a similar point in Ephesians 4:7–16. Each individual Christian has a gift and they must exercise that gift for the greater good. The goal is not motor racing but 'body building'. It is the highest goal possible: the building up of the body of Christ to full unity, maturity and Christlikeness (4:12–16).

Here in 4:7, Paul starts by emphasising how each one of us has been given special gifts of 'grace ... as Christ apportioned it'. The 'grace' he is referring to is not the 'saving grace' of 2:8–9, but is the 'ministry grace' that he, Paul, has spoken about concerning his own life in 3:2, 7–8, but now is applying to every single believer. So let's pause and consider this stunning revelation: if you are a Christian you are not only 'saved' by grace and 'sustained' by grace, but are also 'gifted' by grace for ministry. This foundational truth is not based on just this one text, but is confirmed many times throughout the New Testament (see Rom. 12:3–8; 1 Cor. 12:7–11; 12:28–31; 1 Pet. 4:10–11).

In the light of this huge privilege and high calling, it is a tragedy that in many churches many are *not* exercising their gifts. You may be one of them. The reasons for this are numerous. In some instances it is due to an unbiblical and unhealthy distinction between 'clergy' and 'laity', which can rob individual believers of a sense of calling to ministry (see Day 12). In other situations, it's simply that people lack teaching on the subject of spiritual gifts and are therefore unaware that God has gifted *them* and called *them* to ministry. However, sometimes the problem is more down to the individuals themselves: through a combination of low self-esteem, comparison with others, over-busyness, selfishness or even laziness, we can all fail to exercise our God-given gifts. I saw this caption on a church board:

'CH… CH… What's missing? UR'

You may be 'in' church, but effectively you are 'missing' through the non-use of the gift or gifts that God has given you.

So, how then do we discover what gift or gifts God has given us? In Day 37 of *Transformed Life* I emphasise three main pathways for discovering one's spiritual gifts. The first is through revelation: the Lord will speak to you in various ways, and reveal to you who He has made you to be, and what are your specific gifts. The second is through consultation: as you seek input from mature spiritual leaders, and avail yourself of various spiritual gifts surveys and personality profiles, your gifts will become clearer. The third, and in my experience the most common way, is by experimentation: we discover our gifts by beginning to use them!

REFLECT AND RESPOND

- At the start of this week, take time to thank God for the unique gifts He has given you. Acknowledge before Him that you didn't earn them or deserve them and that they were not your decision but His.

- Consider whether there are any gifts that are lying dormant in you. Ask for God's help in discerning who He made you to be and when and how to begin using these gifts.

MEMORY VERSE

'But to each one of us grace has been given as Christ apportioned it.'

EPHESIANS 4:7

YOU HAVE A GIFT FROM THE ASCENDED JESUS!

'This is why it says: "When he ascended on high, he took many captives and gave gifts to his people." (What does "he ascended" mean except that he also descended to the lower, earthly regions? He who descended is the very one who ascended higher than all the heavens, in order to fill the whole universe.)' **EPHESIANS 4:8–10**

As a young man, Winston Churchill bent down beside a stream to pick up a stick, when the pocket-watch in his breast pocket slipped out and fell into the stream. He immediately dropped his outer garments and jumped in to try to retrieve it. After a few minutes without success he hired 23 men from his infantry detachment to dig a new route from the part of the stream in which he was sure the watch had fallen. He then hired a military fire engine to drain the area and found his rusted and broken watch at the bottom. On finding it, he picked it up and sent it for repair. Why did he go to such great lengths to retrieve the watch? *It was a gift from his father.*[1]

If Churchill so valued a pocket watch from his father, how much more should we value special, life-transforming gifts that we have been given by our heavenly Father in and through His Son, Jesus Christ. This is at the heart of our text today. In verse 7 we have seen that Paul emphasises that each of us has received a gift, 'as Christ apportioned it'. Here, in 4:8–10, he unpacks this further by highlighting that the gifts come from the *ascended* Christ. Paul grounds his assertion by quoting from Psalm 68:18. In its original context, this refers to God triumphantly ascending to Mount Zion, leading defeated 'enemies' and 'receiving gifts' from men.

Here, Paul relates the psalm to Christ defeating His (and our) spiritual enemies, victoriously ascending to heaven and 'giving gifts' to men. Then he makes an additional comment concerning Christ's descent to the 'lower, earthly regions', and to his 'ascent' to a place 'higher than all the heavens'. Much debate surrounds the meaning of Christ's descent. The main traditional view has been that this relates to Christ's descent to hell. The most popular contemporary view is that this refers to His descent to earth in the incarnation. Either way, the key focus is that the one who descended also victoriously ascended to the Father's right hand in glory, and then distributed gifts to His people.

Like Churchill, and even more so, this should dramatically affect our appreciation of our spiritual gifts. First, it means that we should highly value our gifts, since they have been given to us by the ascended Christ Himself. He went to the Father and received gifts to give to us. Second, we need to celebrate our uniqueness and avoid the dangerous snare of comparison. I know from personal experience that comparing myself to others is one of the quickest ways to stop me from faithfully exercising my own gifts. As pastor Robert Madu points out: 'Comparison is the cancer to contentment.'[2] Positively, when you and I are aware of our uniqueness and rejoice in this, we can genuinely celebrate the gifts of others and can start working with them in teams, thus experiencing high degrees of effectiveness and satisfaction in God's service. Third, we need to actually exercise the gifts that we have been given in the service of God and other people. As good stewards, we must use what God has given us.

In the context of Psalm 68 and Ephesians 4, the implication is that as we, the body, faithfully exercise our gifts, Christ, the head, will continue to exercise His Lordship – including enforcing Christ's victory against evil principalities and powers (see 1:20–23 and 6:10–20). In the light of this, our receiving grace gifts for ministry and faithfully exercising those gifts is an issue of not just temporal and temporary significance, but of cosmic and eternal importance! All of this highlights that you and I using the gift or gifts that we have received is vital. As we do so, we honour Christ, we wrestle against evil, and we minister to others – thus fulfilling our God-given destiny.

REFLECT AND RESPOND

- **Think about some of the important people in your life. Consider their spiritual gifts and thank God for the times when their gifts enriched yours. Pray that God would bless them and strengthen them in their journey of faith.**

- **Ask God to forgive and help you if you have fallen into the trap of comparing yourself to others. Invite Him to set you free! And celebrate the unique calling that He has on your life.**

- **Determine to start exercising your gifts in God's service and the service of others.**

MEMORY VERSE

'But to each one of us grace has been given as Christ apportioned it.'
EPHESIANS 4:7

DAY 10

LEADERSHIP

'So Christ himself gave the apostles, the prophets, the evangelists, the pastors and teachers' **EPHESIANS 4:11**

Leadership really matters. In whatever sphere of life – government, education, health, media, finance and church – having the right leaders, in the right roles, leading in the right way, makes a massive difference. This is certainly the case with church. Bill Hybels, pastor of Willow Creek, writes this: 'The local church is the hope of the world, and its future rests primarily in the hands of its leaders.'[1]

This is not, of course, to suddenly downplay the role of *every* believer: in fact this whole passage in 4:7–16 is focusing on the role that each one of us has to play. But it is important that we recognise and honour those with specific leadership gifts, because they have the vital role of equipping all believers for the work of the ministry (v12). So who are these important 'leaders'? They are 'gifts' to the body of Christ, given by the ascended Christ (see 4:8–10). The 'he' here in verse 11 is Christ, emphasising His sovereignty in the gracing of these particular people. It's important to note that there is no suggestion that those mentioned here in 4:11 are a complete list. In fact, 1 Corinthians 12:28–29 doesn't mention pastors and evangelists, but includes apostles, prophets and teachers, workers of miracles, those having gifts of healing, those able to help others, those with gifts of administration, and those speaking in different kinds of tongues. That said, there does seem to be something significant about the 'offices' of Ephesians 4:11 and their particular leadership role in equipping everyone else for their ministry. So, let's look briefly at each in turn.

First mentioned are apostles, literally 'sent ones'. It's important to first acknowledge the unique role of the 12 apostles of Jesus, and the apostle Paul (who through personal revelation had a particular role in the initial establishing of the Church), including for a number of them, the writing of the New Testament. However, the obvious presence of *other* New Testament apostles, such as Barnabas (Acts 13:2–4; 14:4), along with this text here in Ephesians 4:11, serves to emphasise that apostles were and are *still* vital for the healthy functioning of the Church throughout history. In the words of one commentator: 'Christ is continuing to give these leaders to the church for the equipping of the individual members and facilitating their growth to maturity'.[2] So what are these 'sent ones' sent to do? In general terms they are called to go and preach the gospel and establish churches, laying healthy foundations for the future growth of individual believers and the corporate body.

Second in the list are prophets. This refers not to the Old Testament prophets but to new covenant people through whom God still speaks. Their role includes the broader gift of prophecy, where people speak to others 'for their strengthening, encouragement and comfort' (1 Cor. 4:3). However, New Testament prophets are also there to operate in a leadership role, alongside apostles, in helping to establish healthy foundations in the Church, as well as to equip others to function effectively in the whole arena of prophetic ministry.

Third, there are the evangelists. Given that part of the role of the apostles would have been to go and proclaim the gospel in new areas where they would establish churches, 'the evangelists were probably those who remained in the local churches and continued to make known the gospel to those in the city or region who still had not heard'.[3] However, picking up on 4:11–12, the evangelists were not just called to preach the gospel, but also to equip believers to more effectively share their faith.

Fourth, there are pastors. Although some would suggest that these people are linked grammatically to next in the list, teachers, there is strong evidence that these gifts, though often closely linked, are intended to be viewed separately. In spite of its popularity as a title for those in ministry, the term 'pastor' or shepherd is only used here in the New Testament as a term for ministry, although Paul does use the imagery of shepherding one other time (Acts 20:28–29) with the emphasis on leaders who exercise 'a great deal of care, concern, and godly leadership'.[4]

Fifth, there are teachers. Teaching was a responsibility of the pastors and was a qualification for someone who serves as an overseer or elder. Apostles also exercised a foundational teaching role, so it may be that 'teachers' were to follow up by providing ongoing teaching.

All of this highlights that if we want to have healthy believers and churches, we need to make room for and embrace what is sometimes known as the 'five-fold' ministry of apostles, prophets, evangelists, pastors and teachers. They are sovereignly given to the Church by Jesus Christ.

REFLECT AND RESPOND

- **Today, pray for the leaders in your church. Thank God for the gift that they are. Pray that they would continue to discover and walk in the gifting that they have been given.**

MEMORY VERSE

'But to each one of us grace has been given as Christ apportioned it.'

EPHESIANS 4:7

EVERY MEMBER IN MINISTRY

'to equip the saints for the work of ministry, for building up the body of Christ' **EPHESIANS 4:12 (ESV)**

During the Transformed Life series, I preached on Ephesians 3:1–13 on the subject of 'gifted for service'. As each person arrived on that particular Sunday, they were given a jigsaw piece. They could probably make out enough to see that it contained a part of a wild cat – a lion, tiger, cheetah, leopard or something similar. Then during the message, I unveiled a complete and finished jigsaw puzzle of a huge lion, made up of all the parts of the puzzle. The point was to illustrate that, like a jigsaw piece, each of us has a distinct, unique and vital part to play to make up the whole jigsaw. For us to do this, we first need to see the final picture that we are going to make, and get rightly fitted next to the other pieces!

Here in Ephesians 4:12 Paul begins to give us the final picture, the goal of all ministry, which is 'that the body of Christ may be built up' to full unity, maturity and Christlikeness (4:12–16, see Days 12–14). Each of us are not just pieces of the jigsaw, but members of that body, and each of us has a vital role to play. First, there are the leadership gifts of 4:11, whose job is to 'prepare' or 'equip' everyone else for *their* work of ministry. It's worth pausing and emphasising this. Sometimes when people decide to devote themselves to full-time work within the Church they are described as 'going into the ministry'. Unfortunately, this term can obscure the much broader truth revealed here, which is that *every* believer in Christ ('God's people' in the NIV; 'the saints' in the ESV) is called to the ministry, whether full-time or part-time.

In order to understand why this great revelation has been lost or obscured, it's helpful to understand a bit of simple Church history. As we can see from passages like this in Ephesians, the New Testament era was one where there was a full embracing of every member in ministry. During what is often known as the Middle Ages, sadly this truth was largely replaced by the 'priests', who were the professional clergy, and the rest, known as the 'laity'. In the sixteenth century, during what is known as the Reformation, this distinction was partly removed through the recovery of what was known as the 'priesthood of all believers'. I say partly, because although all believers were recognised as having equal access before God in terms of salvation and their relationship with Him, in practice, the *ministry* aspect of 'priesthood' was not fully restored. For many centuries, including in Reformation-based churches, the ministry remained largely the preserve of 'pastors' or leaders with different titles. Thankfully this is changing. One of the most important restorations of the late twentieth- and early twenty-first-century Church has been the restoration of the 'five-fold' equipping gifts, and with this a growing understanding that every member of the body of Christ is called into ministry.

This doesn't mean that leaders are now unimportant. As we saw yesterday, the 'five-fold' ministries are gifts from the ascended Christ. But the role of the leaders is not so much to *do* the ministry, as to *equip others* for the work of the ministry.

In the light of this, it is vital that we properly understand this word 'equip' (or 'prepare' in the NIV). One aspect of equipping concerns the idea of mending for a purpose. In Matthew 4:21, for example, the word is used to describe the disciples mending their nets for the purpose of preparing them for catching more fish. In a similar way, the 'five-fold' ministry people are to help repair, mend or restore broken lives, as a way of preparing them for effective ministry, including 'catching' others in the loving gospel net! The word 'equipping' was also used for the setting of bones that had become dislocated, so that the limb becomes perfect again.

All of this highlights the huge privilege that you have if you are a believer in Jesus Christ. You are His minister. God has a plan and purpose for you here on planet Earth, which includes you being 'equipped' (repaired and trained) for service. This service is to be directed towards the greatest goal possible: the building up of the Church of Jesus Christ.

REFLECT AND RESPOND

- **Do you currently see church 'ministry' as a duty or a privilege?**

- **Take some time to meditate on today's scripture. Ask for God's strength if you feel tired. Ask for His vision if you feel disillusioned. Ask for His grace if you feel misunderstood. Set your heart on Jesus and ask for His enabling to remain faithful to Him and His Church.**

- **Pray that God would keep your passion alive. Dedicate your ministry afresh to Him today and thank Him that He has chosen you to be His minister!**

MEMORY VERSE

'But to each one of us grace has been given as Christ apportioned it.'
EPHESIANS 4:7

THE HIGH GOAL
OF MINISTRY

'so that the body of Christ may be built up, until we all reach unity in the faith and in the knowledge of the Son of God and become mature, attaining to the whole measure of the fullness of Christ.' **EPHESIANS 4:12–13**

Many people think of their lives a bit like a ladder, with the goal to keep taking steps higher to the ultimate goal of success. The only problem is that, in the words of Steven Covey, 'If the ladder is not leaning against the right wall, every step we take just gets us to the wrong place faster'[1]. So, what is the right goal for our lives? While each of us will have different gifts, ministries and career paths, we all have one common high God-designed goal which, in the words of the old creed, 'is to glorify God and enjoy him forever'. So, what does it mean to glorify God? Author and pastor John Piper highlights that we are to glorify God '*by* enjoying Him forever'[2]. Here, in Ephesians 4:12–13, we can see that living for God's glory involves living for the fame of His Son Jesus Christ, and for the building up of His body, the Church. Then through a unified, mature and Christlike Church, His glory can be revealed and multitudes will be transformed. That's a truly God-glorifying and glorious goal!

So what does that look like in practice? It means that all our ministry in serving others (see Day 11) is directed towards this building up or edifying of the body of Christ, both internally and externally. As Klyne

Snodgrass writes: 'The focus is mostly on internal strengthening of the church, but building up of the church by reaching out to unbelievers is also included'.[3]

As the Church grows and is built, so we will together attain to 'the unity in the faith and in the knowledge of the Son of God' (4:13). Here we see something of the tension between the 'already' and the 'not yet' of the Christian life. We have already been given a unity in the Spirit that we are to *maintain* (4:3). Yet we are to continue to pursue this as a high goal, so that we will *attain* this more completely. We already have 'one faith' (4:5), yet its oneness is yet to be fully appropriated. We already have a unity based on our 'knowledge of the Son of God', but we must still grow in this personal, experiential knowledge of Him (see 1:9–10,17–19; 3:16–19). When it comes to 'knowing' Christ in this way, none of us have arrived, but we must all get to know more of Him in a deep and personal way, as He knows and loves us fully.

The ultimate goal of this growth in united faith and knowledge of the Son of God is that the body will 'mature'. This is not referring so much to our individual maturity, although this is obviously important, but rather the maturity of the Church as a whole. Lloyd-Jones summarises it this way: 'God's grand purpose and programme is that the church should be perfect … The perfect man consists not only of the Head Himself, Jesus Christ, who is always perfect, but also of us who form the limbs and individual parts the body … That body … is not going to perfect until every single part and portion is perfect.'[4]

This unity and maturity will result in the body becoming fully Christlike: 'attaining to the whole measure of the fullness of Christ' (4:13). What a high and glorious goal – far greater than any other. Let's give our lives, our gifts and our ministries for this great purpose!

REFLECT AND RESPOND

- Are you living for the high goal of ministry or simply the by-products like recognition and praise for hard work, or people thinking highly of you?

- In what ways can you get to know Jesus more?

- Pray that your church and the wider global Church would continue to move forwards towards perfect unity and maturity.

MEMORY VERSE

'But to each one of us grace has been given as Christ apportioned it.'

EPHESIANS 4:7

GROWING UP

'Then we will no longer be infants, tossed back and forth by the waves, and blown here and there by every wind of teaching and by the cunning and craftiness of people in their deceitful scheming. Instead, speaking the truth in love, we will grow to become in every respect the mature body of him who is the head, that is, Christ.' **EPHESIANS 4:14–15**

I don't know if you have ever had anyone say to you these words: 'Grow up!' I certainly have! Well, here Paul is saying that when every member is playing his or her part in the ministry then the body of Christ will be built up in unity, maturity, and Christlikeness, and then we will 'no longer be infants' but will instead 'we are to *grow up* into in every way him who is the head, into, Christ' (ESV, my emphasis).

The fact that Paul says that we will 'no longer be infants' highlights that when we first come to Christ we are not grown up spiritually. Elsewhere in the New Testament we see that to become a Christian means for us to be born again (John 3:1–8) and that we start out as 'new born babies' who need the 'milk' of the Word so that we can grow (1 Pet. 2:2). From children, we become young adults and then spiritual parents ourselves (see 1 John 2:12–13). This obvious fact serves to emphasise that becoming a Christian is just the beginning of a lifelong journey of spiritual growth and transformation.

Here in 4:14–15, Paul highlights that one of the primary keys to us growing up into Christ, is the importance of not being deceived by false teaching, but of speaking and living the truth. This is clearly of key significance so let's unpack both the negative and positive aspects in turn.

First, if we are to no longer be infants, we must not allow ourselves to be swayed by false teaching. Paul uses a couple of images to describe this state of infancy: being tossed around by the waves and being blown by the wind – both images describe a state of immaturity and insecurity, and a vulnerability to deception. This is not just a first-century problem. As Terry Virgo points out: 'Christians are vulnerable to doctrinal error as much in our day as they were in Paul's. Indeed through widespread accessibility of books, radio and television a virtual smorgasbord of novel doctrine is available to tempt the pallet (and maybe poison the soul)'.[1] Over a decade since Terry was writing, one might add that novel doctrines are all the more accessible through the web and social media. Notwithstanding the considerable benefits of accessing good teaching online, it does highlight that we need to be especially discerning in what teaching we allow ourselves to be influenced by.

Second, we are called to grow up, by 'speaking the truth in love'. The word 'speaking' doesn't appear in the original, so this could be literally translated '*truthing* it in love'. It would surely include speaking the truth, but has the wider sense of *living* the truth. As every member seeks to operate under the sovereignty of the ascended Christ, and do his or her ministry to build up the body, this will include a teaching and a lifestyle that are in accord with the truth that is in Christ (see 4:20). Notice though that it is speaking the truth 'in love'. This provides the necessary balance and antidote to people using the supposed 'truth' to spend their whole time trying to 'correct error', including through social media – often in a distinctly un-loving way!

The real context here seems to be that the local church is to be seen as a community that is teaching and living the truth in love – with the goal of bringing the Church to unity, maturity and Christlikeness.

REFLECT AND RESPOND

- Are there any ways in which you need to 'grow up' spiritually?

- Determine not to be someone who is prone to listen to and be influenced by false teaching, but instead someone who seeks to speak and live the truth of Christ, mentoring others in the same way.

MEMORY VERSE

'But to each one of us grace has been given as Christ apportioned it.'

EPHESIANS 4:7

EVERY PART WORKING

'From him the whole body, joined and held together by every supporting ligament, grows and builds itself up in love, as each part does its work.' **EPHESIANS 4:16**

I know from painful experience the importance of ligaments. I was in my early twenties, studying for my thesis and doing part-time teaching at a local Oxford school. I was playing on the staff side in a 'friendly' match against the boys, when one of the boys decided I was playing a bit too well! He came from behind and caught my knee in a scissor-like movement. The moment he did I knew something was wrong. I got up, and immediately my whole knee buckled. I went to surgery to find that my cruciate ligaments had snapped. For months afterwards I was aware of how vital those small ligaments were.

Here, Paul uses the image of ligaments to emphasise how vital we all are as individual parts of the body of Christ. In verse 15 Paul has just told us that it is from Christ, the head, that the 'whole body' gets its connection and proper functioning. Here in 4:16, he moves on to emphasise the importance of all the parts functioning, since the body is also 'joined and held together by every supporting ligament'. Hence, in this concluding verse, which summarises the main message of this whole passage (4:7–16), Paul highlights once again the importance of every member playing his or her part, with the result that the body 'grows and builds itself up in love', finishing the sentence with the telling phrase 'as each part does its work'. It is so important that we don't allow any relational 'tears' to hinder us. It's equally vital that we don't despise either our own gifts or those of others as somehow insignificant. Like ligaments, we all have a 'crucial' role to play!

This all goes to highlight the main theme of this week, which is the importance of *every* member of the body functioning in ministry. I remember a number of years ago hearing a church leader talk about the 80/20 principle as something that we simply have to accept in church life. The 80/20 principle is the idea that 80% of the work in any given organisation is done by 20% of the people. Now, while this may be the case in many organisations, including sadly in many churches, it is *not* a status quo that we can or should accept. Rather, we must embrace with a passion the call for every member to be actively involved in ministry.

Having every member in ministry involves a number of things. As we saw in Day 8, it is based on the fact that everyone has a special grace gift or gift. These gifts are special since they come from the ascended Christ Himself (Day 9). Some are called with particular leadership gifts, but their job is not to do all the ministry, but to equip everyone else for their work of ministry (Days 10–11). This ministry has the high goal of building up the body of Christ (Day 12), which is accomplished through speaking the truth in love.

In case by now the message isn't clear, let me restate: God has called *you* to ministry. It is vital that you embrace this call: both for your own sense of significance and destiny in Christ, but also because you have a critical part to play in the greatest plan on the planet – the building up of a unified, mature and Christlike Church.

REFLECT AND RESPOND

- How can you build others up in love while you are serving?

- Consider once again what God has called you to and resolve to act.

MEMORY VERSE

'But to each one of us grace has been given as Christ apportioned it.'

EPHESIANS 4:7

WEEK 3
PURITY

'So I tell you this, and insist on it in the Lord, that you must no longer live as the Gentiles do, in the futility of their thinking. They are darkened in their understanding and separated from the life of God because of the ignorance that is in them due to the hardening of their hearts. Having lost all sensitivity, they have given themselves over to sensuality so as to indulge in every kind of impurity, and they are full of greed.

That, however, is not the way of life you learned when you heard about Christ and were taught in him in accordance with the truth that is in Jesus. You were taught, with regard to your former way of life, to put off your old self, which is being corrupted by its deceitful desires; to be made new in the attitude of your minds; and to put on the new self, created to be like God in true righteousness and holiness.

Therefore each of you must put off falsehood and speak truthfully to your neighbour, for we are all members of one body. "In your anger do not sin": do not let the sun go down while you are still angry, and do not give the devil a foothold. Anyone who has been stealing must steal no longer, but must work, doing something useful with their own hands, that they may have something to share with those in need.

Do not let any unwholesome talk come out of your mouths, but only what is helpful for building others up according to their needs, that it may benefit those who listen. And do not grieve the Holy Spirit of God, with whom you were sealed for the day of redemption. Get rid of all bitterness, rage and anger, brawling and slander, along with every form of malice. Be kind and compassionate to one another, forgiving each other, just as in Christ God forgave you.'

EPHESIANS 4:17–32

DON'T LIVE LIKE YOU USED TO!

'So I tell you this, and insist on it in the Lord, that you must no longer live as the Gentiles do, in the futility of their thinking. They are darkened in their understanding and separated from the life of God because of the ignorance that is in them due to the hardening of their hearts. Having lost all sensitivity, they have given themselves over to sensuality so as to indulge in every kind of impurity, and they are full of greed.' **EPHESIANS 4:17–19**

One of the defining moments of my life came in the summer term of my first year at university. I had recently become a Christian and had already begun to live for God, to meet with other Christians and grow in my faith. However, I also tried to keep in with my rugby-playing, beer-drinking friends that I had gravitated towards before my conversion. So, on one occasion I went out with this group as before. Although I found myself uncomfortable with the heavy drinking and the crude singing, I ended up drinking so much that the evening ended with my acting roughly towards an unsuspecting bystander behind a burger van in the centre of Oxford! I went home embarrassed and shocked at my behaviour and realised that if I was to become a fully devoted follower of Christ, I couldn't continue trying to keep a foot in both camps. Without rejecting those previous friends or ending up in a Christian ghetto, I made a decision that I couldn't continue to live in any way that compromised my newfound faith.

I could have done with reading and digesting the implications of Ephesians 4:17–32, prior to that 'sobering' incident. Paul starts this new section by exhorting those who are now in Christ to 'no longer live as the Gentiles do'. He then unpacks what the typical pagan life looks like (4:17–19), before giving encouragement to live in the new life and not the old (4:20–24), concluding with five key examples of what that looks like in practice (4:25–32). Here in 4:17–19 he starts with four key phrases that highlight why we must live differently (v17), before painting in more detail what a pre-Christian life is typified by.

First, in 4:17, Paul starts his call to a life of purity, as with the call to unity (4:1), by using the key word 'so' or 'therefore'. It's easy to pass over this, but it's important that we don't do so. It highlights that our call to live out our new life is based firmly on what God has already done for us in Christ. It is precisely because we have a new identity, place of belonging and purpose in Christ that we can and must live differently.

Second, Paul highlights the weightiness of his words and the seriousness of this call by restating once more (as in 4:1) that he has the Lord's authority to call us to this life of purity: 'I … insist on it in the Lord'. Thus he is emphasising that we must not be casual or half-hearted in our response to our great calling.

Third, our Christian life is meant to affect every aspect of our lives. When he says that we are to 'no longer live as the Gentiles do', the word used is literally to no longer 'walk' as they do. This highlights that we are to be transformed in every part of our life and lifestyle.

Fourth, he uses a strong phrase to convey what he considers to be a pre-Christian way of living: 'the futility of their thinking'. 'Futility' is the same word often translated in the book of Ecclesiastes as 'meaninglessness'. At the time, such a position would have caused offence amongst many who were not yet Christians. Some, such as the Stoics, thought they were living moral and upright lives. But Paul's statement deliberately includes not just those who are obviously living disordered, immoral lives, but also those who considered themselves upright, but didn't have God as their focal point.

Lloyd-Jones puts it this way: 'Life without Christ is always empty, it is always vain, it takes from you, it takes out of you, and it leaves you at the end the empty husk. It leaves you exhausted, with nothing to lean on, nothing to be proud of, and nothing whatsoever to look forward to.'[1]

Then, in verses 18–19, Paul proceeds to emphasise the importance of living differently by piling on descriptions of the futility of this pre-Christian mindset:

- a darkened understanding
- being alienated from the life of God
- being ignorant of God
- due to a hardening of the heart

This self-centred mindset and calloused heart condition has fatal consequences. Such people:

- have lost all sensitivity
- have given themselves over to sensuality
- have a continual lust for more

Why this stark language? Because Paul is wanting to challenge his readers to make a radical break with their past lifestyle and the surrounding culture. This is equally relevant today. In the West we live in a culture that is increasingly post-Christian, is in many ways anti-Christian and is therefore getting closer again to the pre-Christian culture of the first century. The message is clear: now that we are in Christ, we must break from the past and from the value system of the world around us. I discovered this in the aftermath of the incident at the burger van. You may need to do a similar re-evaluation of your life today.

REFLECT AND RESPOND

- As you pause and reflect on this sobering passage of the Bible, take a moment to prayerfully ask the Lord to reveal to you any areas where you may be compromising.

- Ask God to forgive you for any areas of compromise, and invite the Holy Spirit to come and help you as you undertake a life of purity.

MEMORY VERSE

'put off your old self ... put on the new self, created to be like God in true righteousness and holiness.'

EPHESIANS 4:22,24

THE NEW LIFE IN CHRIST

'That, however, is not the way of life you learned when you heard about Christ and were taught in him in accordance with the truth that is in Jesus. You were taught, with regard to your former way of life, to put off your old self, which is being corrupted by its deceitful desires; to be made new in the attitude of your minds; and to put on the new self, created to be like God in true righteousness and holiness.' **EPHESIANS 4:20–24**

Putting off the old. Putting on the new.

Imagine a man who was a poacher, who was one day caught by the head gamekeeper and sent to prison. In prison he turns his life around and decides to put his knowledge of wildlife to better use by training to become a gamekeeper himself. On his release, the head gamekeeper takes pity on him and gives him a job on the estate he used to poach from. He no longer wears his poacher's coat, but instead wears a brand new gamekeeper's coat. Very grateful for his opportunity, he goes about his job with great diligence.

One day, whilst getting ready in his hut, he decides to try on his old coat again just to see how it feels. He stands before the mirror and lots of the old feelings come back. Deep down he knows his new position is much better; standing in the old coat, he remembers the excitement of sneaking around, of lying when asked what he was doing, of stealing from the estate. Then with a start, he turns and notices the head gamekeeper is watching him. He looks embarrassed and ashamed, but the head gamekeeper does not shout at him, but rather very kindly says to him, 'Put on your new coat.' We understand what is happening. The head gamekeeper is not just calling for a wardrobe change. He is saying, 'Drop all allegiances to the old ways of living, sneaking around, lying about what you are up to, breaking the law, stealing from the estate. You have a new position and identity now. It has been given to you; be grateful and live up to it.'

This is similar to what Paul is saying to us in Ephesians 4:20–24: you have been made new, so put off the old and put on the new. As a continuation of 4:17–19, where he has highlighted the futility of our old lives outside of Christ, he starts by making the telling point: 'You, however, did not come to know Christ that way' (4:20, NIV 1984). The phrase 'know Christ' (literally 'learned Christ') is referring to a personal, experiential knowledge *of Christ*, which would have also included teaching *about Christ* – including instruction about His person, His redemptive work, our new identity in Him and how we are to live now as a result. This ethical emphasis is particularly what Paul has in mind here in 4:22–24. In the words of John Stott: 'to "learn Christ" is to grasp the new creation which he has made possible, and the entirely new life which results from it. It is nothing less than putting off our old humanity like a rotten garment and putting on like clean clothing the new humanity recreated in God's image.'[1]

The key question is when does this putting off and putting on take place, and how does it apply to our lives? Some commentators refer to the parallel passage in Colossians 3:9–10, and suggest that Paul is reminding us of the radical change that *has already* taken place, through our 'conversion' (our human response of repentance and rebirth), and 're-creation' (God's miracle of new birth). This transformation involved no longer living in our fallen or sinful nature, but receiving our new nature in Christ, 'fresh, beautiful and vigorous, like God'.[2]

Sandwiched between the contrasting portraits of what has already happened through the putting off of the old (v22) and the putting on of the new (v24) is the practical exhortation to 'be made new in the attitude of your minds' (v23). This is written in the present infinitive and indicates the need for a continuous inward renewal. It is a deliberate re-emphasis on the mind and a contrast to the 'futile' thinking of 4:17–19.

This renewing of the 'attitude' (literally 'spirit') of our minds is one of the primary ongoing works of the Holy Spirit in our lives that requires our full co-operation. Put simply, if we want to live in the good of having put off the old and put on the new, we must allow the Spirit to renew our minds on a daily, even a continual basis!

REFLECT AND RESPOND

- **Are there any areas of your life where you keep finding yourself falling back into your 'old' nature, either in your actions or your ways of thinking? How would your life be different if you lived fully within the new nature that God has designed for you?**

- **Choose today to practically start co-operating with the Holy Spirit in the vital task of renewing your mind. Take extra time not just to read these studies but to meditate on key truths that God has spoken to you about. Get the Word into your mind, heart and mouth (see Josh. 1:8) and watch how the Spirit renews your thinking.**

MEMORY VERSE

'put off your old self … put on the new self, created to be like God in true righteousness and holiness.'
EPHESIANS 4:22,24

DON'T LIE, SPEAK THE TRUTH

'Therefore each of you must put off falsehood and speak truthfully to your neighbour, for we are all members of one body.' **EPHESIANS 4:25**

There is a story of the great American President, George Washington, cutting down with a hatchet what was, unbeknown to him, his father's favourite cherry tree. When his father came home and saw what had happened he was very angry and questioned George, who replied, 'I cannot tell a lie, Father, you know I cannot tell a lie! I did cut it with my little hatchet.' His father's anger disappeared, he embraced the boy and told him telling the truth was worth more to him than a thousand trees. Well, it is a lovely story. It is also not true! It was, ironically, an invention of Washington's biographer, whose intention was to show that Washington's great achievements came from his great virtues and to inspire others to be like him. To some degree it has worked. The cherry tree myth has endured and Washington's legacy has been inspirational. The story also serves to illustrate that at the heart of good character and integrity is the rejection of lying and the need to tell the truth.

Here in Ephesians 4:25, Paul highlights that as Christ-followers called to live the new life, we must 'put off falsehood and speak truthfully'. Significantly, this is the first of a series of exhortations (see 4:25–32) concerning what it looks like practically to live as those who have 'put off' the old self and 'put on' the new self (4:22–24). It is worth noting from the outset that this and all the other exhortations concern our horizontal relationship with others. Transformed living starts with our relationship with the Lord, but must affect also our relationship with others.

So why does Paul start with this emphasis on lies and truth? It seems, in part, because he is re-emphasising the contrast that he has made in 4:17–24 between the deception or the big 'lie' of the pagan lifestyle and the 'truth' that is in Jesus. Here he now urges them to 'put off all falsehood and speak truthfully'.

Throughout Scripture, God's hatred for lying is evident (see Prov. 6:16–17; 12:19,22; 20:17; 21:6; Rev. 21:7–8; 21:27; 22:15). Significantly, from the Fall onwards, Satan is characterised by deception and even called the 'father of lies'. Similarly, God is a God of truth, Jesus came from God 'full of grace and truth' (John 1:14) and the Holy Spirit is called the Spirit of truth.

But here in Ephesians 4:25, this call to reject all falsehood and speak the truth seems to be based on a more practical and relational reason, which is that 'we are all members of one body'. Given Paul's passion for and primary concern for the unity of the 'one body' (4:3–4), here he is urgently stressing the need for the rejection of falsehood and the embracing of truth, because without this there is no real unity. There is nothing that will more quickly destroy trust than a lack of truth. How many relationships in the home, the workplace or church have been seriously undermined by a lack of trust due to a lack of or absence of truthfulness? Read the words of Martyn Lloyd-Jones: 'If only lying could be entirely banished, what loads would be lifted off minds and hearts! Oh, the havoc caused by lying, the heartbreak, the sadness, the unhappiness, the suffering to innocent people that is caused by this lying. It is no wonder that the Apostle tells us to put it away as the first thing we deal with!'[1]

Therefore, we must be people of the truth, who determine to reject lying, and 'speak the truth in love' (4:15).

REFLECT AND RESPOND

- **If the 'putting off' of lying and the embracing of truthful speech is so foundational, then it is important to pause and ask the Lord to reveal areas where we have not been truthful. Repent of any lies and deception.**

- **Ask the Holy Spirit to empower you to always speak truthfully.**

MEMORY VERSE

'put off your old self … put on the new self, created to be like God in true righteousness and holiness.'

EPHESIANS 4:22,24

DAY 18

DON'T SIN IN YOUR ANGER

'"In your anger do not sin": do not let the sun go down while you are still angry, and do not give the devil a foothold.' **EPHESIANS 4:26–27**

It was to be his swan song. The great Zinedine Zidane had graced the game of football for many years and was undoubtedly one of the best players of his generation and one of the best in history. All was going according to the script as France made their way to the 2006 World Cup final. Drawn after 90 minutes, the game went into extra time. Still drawn after the first half of extra time it went into the second half. With ten minutes to go there was every reason to believe that France could win the game and Zidane might lift the trophy as the crowning glory of his glittering career. However, it wasn't to be. After an exchange of words with Italian defender Marco Materazzi, Zidane lost his temper and headbutted Materazzi. Actually, 'headbutt' is almost too elegant a description – the replay showed him set his shoulders, drop his head and charge at the defender's chest. It really was reminiscent of a raging bull. No sense, no precision, just pure anger! He was sent off, the game went to penalties and Italy won. One sad image of the incident is of Zidane leaving the field of play and passing by the World Cup trophy that he had hoped to lift, not even looking at it. Apparently Zidane said he does not regret the incident. I am not sure I believe him. I wonder whether he replays the moment many times in his mind and pictures himself counting to ten instead. Arguably, anger cost Zidane and France the World Cup. In many areas of life, anger, especially when it becomes habitual, can cost us far more than that.

Here in 4:26–27, in his second practical exhortation concerning putting off the old and putting on the new nature, Paul homes in on the importance of rightly dealing with anger in our lives. First, it's worth acknowledging that not all anger is bad. Here, Paul quotes from Psalm 4:4: 'In your anger do not sin' – literally, 'be angry, and do not sin', acknowledging that there is a time and place for anger. Throughout Scripture we see that God is righteously angry against evil, and we, too, can and sometimes need to get angry at injustice. However, because of our humanity and frailty, anger is something that we find hard to handle. Our anger is often unrighteous and can so easily be borne out of selfish irritation and, left festering, can lead to a seething bitterness, which is hugely destructive towards ourselves and those who may be the targets of our anger.

Paul gives us three warnings about anger:

1. Don't sin when you are angry. Be very alert to how dangerous anger can be and how it is so often rooted in injured pride, malice or animosity.
2. Put a time limit on your anger. The phrase 'do not let the sun go down while you are still angry' picks up on a biblical idea that we need to settle certain things by the end of the day, unresolved anger being one of them. Many married couples have helpfully and literally sought to put this into practice – seeking to resolve conflict and not let it carry on into the next day.
3. Do not give the devil a foothold. Because of the dangers of sinning in our anger, and of the possibility of anger festering, Paul adds a final warning and a consequence of the first two, which is that sinful, unresolved anger can give the devil a foothold. This is an important warning for us to heed. The word 'foothold' is based on the word *topos*, which means 'place'. Writing to the Ephesians,

many of his hearers would have been saved from the influence of evil spiritual powers; here Paul is seeking to encourage them not to go back under spiritual slavery. In chapters 1–3, he has already shown how God, in Christ, has blessed believers with every spiritual blessing in the heavenly realms, and how through Him they have been made alive and seated 'far above' all principalities and powers (see 1:3; 1:20–23; 2:1–6). Yet evil is still present, and we are still in a spiritual battle (see 6:10–20). One of the ways that the devil seeks to get back into the lives of Christians is through sinful, unresolved anger. Hence the importance of this exhortation: '"In your anger do not sin": do not let the sun go down while you are still angry, and do not give the devil a foothold' (4:26–27).

REFLECT AND RESPOND

- **Take a moment to prayerfully ask God to reveal to you any areas where you are holding unrighteous anger. Repent, ask for forgiveness and release His grace to those around you.**

- **Ask God to put a righteous anger in you for the things that He hates (injustice, sin, corruption, greed etc) and ask for His anointing to live a holy life, bringing His light into darkness.**

MEMORY VERSE

'put off your old self … put on the new self, created to be like God in true righteousness and holiness.'
EPHESIANS 4:22,24

DON'T STEAL,
BUT WORK TO GIVE

'Anyone who has been stealing must steal no longer, but must work, doing something useful with their own hands, that they may have something to share with those in need.' **EPHESIANS 4:28**

On Day 1, I referred to the leading character of *Les Misérables*, Jean Valjean. He has spent 19 years in prison for stealing, goes on parole, re-offends, and then his life is transformed by the bishop's willingness to both forgive him and give him even items that he hadn't stolen. From that moment, Valjean devotes himself to hard work, gains wealth and lives the rest of his life generously caring for and giving to others. As well as being a great story, it has echoes here of Ephesians 4:28, with the call to leave behind a life of stealing, to work hard, and to live to give to others.

Let's first start with Paul's prohibition: 'Anyone who has been stealing must steal no longer'. For Paul to write to 'Anyone who has been stealing' indicates that it was more than an isolated incident but a considerable societal problem. It's the same today. Although many of us would hopefully not currently be tempted with more 'obvious' theft like burglary or shop-lifting, we need to be careful that we are not stealing in other ways such as:

- avoiding taxes
- trading dishonestly
- taking things from work
- abusing work time

Having dealt with the negative – 'don't steal' – Paul then highlights the positive, which is the call to work. Throughout Scripture, work is commended as something positive and God-given. Here the emphasis is on 'doing something useful' with one's hands. This is not necessarily referring just to 'manual labour' but to all forms of helpful and productive work. There are many benefits of working in this way. Here, Paul highlights just one: that we might 'have something to share with those in need'.

The contrast between 'stealing' or taking from others, and generously giving or sharing with those in need couldn't be stronger and is a wonderful picture of the contrast between the old life and the new. It highlights that generosity is one of the primary qualities of the new life, and growing in generosity is one of the key ways that we, like Jean Valjean in *Les Misérables*, honour God, serve others and become more like Christ.

Foundational to living generously is the concept of 'stewardship'. It is based on the understanding that everything we have is ultimately a gift from God. This includes the money that we 'earn' since God gave us our lives, our gifts and our talents, which we employ in our work. This means that God is the owner and we are His stewards or managers. Giving to God and others best starts with an acknowledgment that everything we give comes ultimately from God Himself (see 2 Chron. 29). In the Old Testament this giving from one's resources was expressed primarily in two types of giving: returning the 'tithe' (the tenth part) and bringing offerings. From Abraham and Jacob before the Law, to the Law of Moses, through to the book of Malachi, tithing was an established biblical pattern that at least the first 10% of one's income was to be given to God and to the work of the Lord. (Interestingly, in Mal. 3:8–10, the Lord accuses Israel of 'stealing' from Him by withholding tithes and offerings.) Then, there was an established pattern of freewill offerings that included, for example, giving to the poor and helping to fund key projects such as the tabernacle and the Temple. On this Old Testament foundation, Christians are to live lives of radical generosity, based on the total generosity of Jesus towards us (see 2 Cor. 8:9), giving in proportion to our income (1 Cor. 16:1–2) and with expectancy that He will bless and resupply us (see 2 Cor. 9:6–11; Phil. 4:19).

REFLECT AND RESPOND

- **Are you 'stealing' in any way? If so, repent and, where possible, make restitution.**

- **Ask God to help you work hard for His glory. If you are not working and are able to do so, pray that you might get the right job.**

- **Put God first in your finances by bringing a regular 'tithe' into the Lord's house, the local church (see Mal. 3:10; 1 Tim. 3:15). Then, seek to obey the Holy Spirit's prompting by giving above and beyond, both to those in need and to kingdom projects.**

MEMORY VERSE

'put off your old self … put on the new self, created to be like God in true righteousness and holiness.'
EPHESIANS 4:22,24

DON'T SPEAK EVIL; SPEAK WHAT IS GOOD

'Do not let any unwholesome talk come out of your mouths, but only what is helpful for building others up according to their needs, that it may benefit those who listen. And do not grieve the Holy Spirit of God, with whom you were sealed for the day of redemption.' **EPHESIANS 4:29–30**

I remember many years ago learning a lesson that I have never forgotten related to this verse. I was a student, a fairly new Christian, and was being discipled by a church leader. As part of our relationship, I would regularly spend Sunday lunch and afternoon with him and his family. That part was good. What wasn't so good was that invariably the conversation got round to talking critically of other churches in the area. Rather than coming away being built up by our time together, I would regularly come away feeling drained and almost 'sick' inside. I then started to realise that this feeling was not just me, it was the Holy Spirit inside me, who was being 'grieved' by our 'unwholesome talk'. From that moment onwards, and throughout the years, I have sought to watch my words and become more sensitive to the One who lives on the inside.

This is the issue that Paul is addressing here. In continuing his practical exhortations about the need to 'put off the old' and 'put on the new', he emphasises once again the importance of us *changing our speech*. The use of our words and the power of our words are a hugely important emphasis throughout Scripture, and are a recurring theme here in Ephesians 4–6. In 4:15 Paul has already stressed the importance of 'speaking the truth in love'. In 4:25 the focus is on truthful speech, 4:31–32 on loving speech and here in 4:29 on 'unwholesome' and 'helpful' speech. (This same theme of right speaking continues throughout the letter – see 5:4; 5:19–20; 6:17).

Notice here the focus first on the importance of speech in terms of our relationship with others. 'Unwholesome' (meaning rotten or corrupt) speech is contrasted with only speaking 'what is helpful for *building others up according to their needs*' (my emphasis). Here we see that our speech is supposed to be used with others in mind. It highlights that central to transformed living is a call to no longer focus on ourselves.

The importance of replacing unwholesome words with only what is helpful is underscored in the strongest possible terms in verse 30. Here there is a clear link between the need to change our speech and not grieving the Spirit. Paul uses the full title 'Holy Spirit of God', the only time he does so in all his writings, as if to emphasise the importance of his warning. The Spirit is 'holy', hence the importance of holy speech. The Spirit is 'God', so we are talking here about the very presence of God dwelling in and amongst the people of God (see 2:21–22). Moreover, the fact that the Spirit can be 'grieved' refers to the fact that He is relatable and has emotions, someone who can be saddened or vexed. This is supposed to produce in us a holy awe of God's presence, as an exhortation to holiness in this life, *not* a cringing fear of losing our inheritance, since Paul adds that it is through the Spirit that we have been 'sealed for the day of redemption'. In the context of Paul's time, a 'seal' was either the tool or the impression made on a document, creature or object for the purpose of identification or protection. Believers, sealed with the Spirit, are thereby God's possession, and thus guaranteed their final inheritance.

This is not to weaken the seriousness of the call to speak only wholesome words. Rather, it is to emphasise the privilege we have in being sealed with God's very own presence. Returning to our theme of living like royalty (Day 2), it is important to connect our authority in Christ with the power of our words. In life in general, there are multiple examples of how people can be positively or negatively affected by words spoken to them – either by themselves or others. How much more so, then, should those of us who are Christians, now seated with Christ, watch what we say, since our words have the power of life and death (see Prov. 18:21).

REFLECT AND RESPOND

- **Can you think of times when you have been speaking unwholesome words, either consciously or subconsciously? Ask for God's forgiveness where you have grieved His Holy Spirit.**

- **Take some time to pray for any people or situations that you need to. Ask the Holy Spirit to help you become more sensitive to His promptings.**

MEMORY VERSE

'put off your old self ... put on the new self, created to be like God in true righteousness and holiness.'

EPHESIANS 4:22,24

DON'T BE BITTER OR ANGRY; BE KIND, COMPASSIONATE AND FORGIVING

'Get rid of all bitterness, rage and anger, brawling and slander, along with every form of malice. Be kind and compassionate to one another, forgiving each other, just as in Christ God forgave you.' **EPHESIANS 4:31–32**

One of the most haunting creations in literature must be Miss Havisham in Charles Dickens' *Great Expectations*. She was a lady who lived in a decrepit mansion and never left. She was due to marry a young man she had fallen in love with in her youth, but as she was dressing on the day of her wedding, she received a letter from him and in reading it she realised he was a fraud, who planned to take her money and intended to leave her at the altar. From then on, she set her mind to live the rest of her life as a tragic tribute to that moment. The mansion remained exactly as it was, the wedding breakfast set, the clocks stopped at the time she received the letter and she remained in her wedding dress at all times, only accepting a few visitors into the dingy house. She brought up her beautiful adopted daughter Estella to exact revenge on men by becoming a heartbreaker. And when she did then succeed in hurting Pip, the hero of the novel, it brought only more sorrow. Later in the story, Miss Havisham does repent and seeks forgiveness when she sees what she has done to Pip, but only after years of her destructive behaviour.

This is what bitterness can do to us. We can become static; we can live our lives in the memory of something horrible that happened to us in the past. Everything becomes about something we cannot change and we turn in on ourselves and shut others out. Even more damagingly, we can try to exact revenge on others for the wrongs that have been done to us and if we succeed in this it will make us feel worse!

Hence, it is significant that in 4:31, 'bitterness' heads up Paul's list of very harmful characteristics that we are to 'get rid of', followed closely by 'rage and anger, brawling and slander, along with every form of malice'. Verses 31–32 are a continuation of the practical instructions concerning the need to put off the old, put on the new that began in verse 25, but these verses also serve as a reminder of issues that Paul has already dealt with. Hence 'anger' reappears in this list and reminds us of how dangerous unrighteous anger can be (see 4:26–27). Similarly, 'slander' can be seen as a reminder of a particularly harmful form of 'unwholesome speech'. Once again, Paul exhorts us to 'put on' opposite and thoroughly Christlike qualities that are part of the 'new self': notably kindness, compassion and forgiveness. It is important to see once again how these characteristics relate to how we live with others ('one another' or 'each other'), clearly highlighting that Paul's overall concern is for unified, harmonious attitudes within the body of Christ.

However, Paul doesn't just leave us with a list of imperatives: 'get rid of' negative attitudes and 'put on' positive ones. Rather, he gives us the basis for *why* and *how* we are to do this in the final phrase: 'forgiving each other, just as in Christ God forgave you' (4:32). This is so important for us to grasp. The reality is that all of us will get offended and will need to forgive others. Christian pastor and author Bill Hybels seeks to categorise offences as: Minor Offences –

little irritations in life, or slights which can seem big at the time but when we get a right perspective can seem as they really are: 'minor'; Legitimate Wounds that require resolution and healing, and thirdly, Life-shattering Injustices similar to or even worse than Miss Havisham experienced.[1] Whatever 'category' of offence we have experienced, the basis for us to forgive others and be free is the fact that in Christ God has forgiven us freely of an even greater and un-payable debt (see Matt. 18:22–35).

REFLECT AND RESPOND

- **Take some time today to remember what Christ has done for you. Why not reread one of the Gospel accounts of the crucifixion, or find a song or hymn that enables you to 'survey the wondrous cross' and meditate on the grace and forgiveness God has shown you.**

- **Make a choice to forgive (or, in the case of serious offences, to start on the journey of forgiving) those who have hurt you.**

- **Invite the Lord, either on your own or through the prayers of others, to set you free from all bitterness, rage and anger. Ask the Holy Spirit to clothe you with kindness and compassion.**

MEMORY VERSE

'put off your old self … put on the new self, created to be like God in true righteousness and holiness.'

EPHESIANS 4:22,24

WEEK 4
LIVE IN LOVE AND LIGHT

'Follow God's example, therefore, as dearly loved children and live a life of love, just as Christ loved us and gave himself up for us as a fragrant offering and sacrifice to God.

But among you there must not be even a hint of sexual immorality, or of any kind of impurity, or of greed, because these are improper for God's holy people. Nor should there be obscenity, foolish talk or coarse joking, which are out of place, but rather thanksgiving. For of this you can be sure: no immoral, impure or greedy person – such a person is an idolater – has any inheritance in the kingdom of Christ and of God. Let no one deceive you with empty words, for because of such things God's wrath comes on those who are disobedient. Therefore do not be partners with them.

For you were once darkness, but now you are light in the Lord. Live as children of light (for the fruit of the light consists in all goodness, righteousness and truth) and find out what pleases the Lord.

Have nothing to do with the fruitless deeds of darkness, but rather expose them. It is shameful even to mention what the disobedient do in secret. But everything exposed by the light becomes visible – and everything that is illuminated becomes a light. This is why it is said: "Wake up, sleeper, rise from the dead, and Christ will shine on you."'

EPHESIANS 5:1–14

LIVE A LIFE OF LOVE

'Be imitators of God, therefore, as dearly loved children and live a life of love, just as Christ loved us and gave himself up for us as a fragrant offering and sacrifice to God.' **EPHESIANS 5:1–2 (NIV 1984)**

I love the way that children so easily and naturally imitate. For example, when our daughter Annabel was at primary school, she was so taken with one of her Year 3 teachers that her favourite game at home was playing teacher. She would make up her own register, and would call out the names of the children in her class, either encouraging or scolding them as in a real lesson. When asked what she wanted to be when she grew up, her reply was: 'A mummy, a teacher and a driver.' Well, she is married, she has learned to drive and she is now enjoying being a primary school teacher. There is considerable power in imitation!

Here, Paul calls us to imitation of the highest order: 'Be imitators of God … and live a life of love'. Obviously we can't fully become God-like. There are certain incommunicable attributes of God such as omnipresence, omniscience and omnipotence that He alone possesses and that we are not called to imitate! Yet there are certain communicable aspects of God's nature that we are called to imitate and embrace, such as holiness and the fruit of the Spirit listed in Galatians 5:22–23, foremost of which is mentioned here in Ephesians 5:2: love.

This call to imitate God and 'live a life of love' is in many ways the highpoint of our calling to live out our new life in Christ.

The pre-eminence of living a life of love is both very significant and is consistent with what Paul teaches elsewhere. For example, in Romans 13:8–10 he highlights that if we love others, we will have fulfilled the moral law, since love does no harm to its neighbour. Hence, in the context of Ephesians, we won't succumb to the sins laid out in the previous section (4:25–32): if we love, we won't lie, steal, be unrighteously angry, speak unwholesome words, or be bitter and unforgiving. Rather, if we love others, we will speak the truth, give, be kind, be compassionate and be forgiving.

So how can we live out this high calling to be like God, especially by loving others? First, it's crucial to grasp that we are called to love as 'dearly loved children'. This is based on the revelation that we have already received from Ephesians 1–3. God the Father loved us from eternity and predestined us to be adopted in His family (1:4–5). Then 'because of his great love for us' he sent His Son to rescue us, to die and rise again for us, so that we might be raised up from our spiritual death (2:4–5). This love is now a present reality to us, and something that we can personally experience through the strengthening of the Holy Spirit and the indwelling of Christ (3:17–19). It is so important that we understand what God in His love has done for us, and that we pray regularly for others to experience that love. Put simply, we *can* love, because we *are* loved.

Then Paul goes on to highlight what this love actually looks like. It's clearly not a mushy, sentimental, shallow love, but a radical, practical and deep love such as that expressed by Jesus Christ, who 'loved us and gave himself up for us as a fragrant offering and sacrifice to God'. We are to live a life of love 'just as' Christ sacrificially loved us!

Here's an illustration from *Our Daily Bread II*: 'During the 17th century, Oliver Cromwell, Lord Protector of England, sentenced a soldier to be shot for his crimes. The execution was to take place at the ringing of the evening curfew bell. However, the bell did not sound. The soldier's fiancé had climbed into the belfry and clung to the great clapper of the bell to prevent it from striking. When she was summoned by Cromwell to account for her actions, she wept as she showed him her bruised and bleeding hands. Cromwell's heart was touched and he said, "Your lover shall live because of your sacrifice. Curfew shall not ring tonight!"[1] In a similar but far greater way, Christ loved each and every one us, giving not just His hands but also His feet, His whole body, His very life to save us.

Our high calling as Christians is therefore to love as we've been loved.

REFLECT AND RESPOND

- **In the light of this high call to be 'imitators of God' and to 'live a life of love', spend some extra time today remembering, receiving and embracing the love of the Father, Son and Holy Spirit.**

- **Ask God to forgive you for your lack of love at times (we can all pray this!).**

- **Is there anyone, particularly, who you need to start practically showing greater love towards? Your spouse, your family, your neighbours, work colleagues, fellow church members? All of the above? Invite the Lord to fill you anew and to empower you to love as He loves.**

MEMORY VERSE

'Be imitators of God, therefore, as dearly loved children and live a life of love, just as Christ loved us and gave himself up for us as a fragrant offering and sacrifice to God.'

EPHESIANS 5:1–2 (NIV 1984)

SHUN SEXUAL IMMORALITY AND GREED

'But among you there must not be even a hint of sexual immorality, or of any kind of impurity, or of greed, because these are improper for God's holy people.' **EPHESIANS 5:3**

Imagine one of those long and winding roads that snake down a mountainside. If you were driving and you were concerned about veering off the road, what would you do? Would you go right up to the edge of the road and peer out the window at the sheer drop beneath you, your wheels teetering over the edge? No – if you value your life you would drive up as close to the mountainside as you possibly could, because the dangers are all too obvious.

Here in Ephesians 5:3, Paul highlights the vital importance of staying as far away from the dangers of sin as possible, particularly from all forms of sexual immorality and greed: 'there must not be *even a hint* of sexual immorality, or of any kind of impurity, or of greed' (my emphasis). He is saying, don't get close to the edge, don't flirt with danger, but stay as far away as possible, since the stakes are incredibly high.

The first warning is against sexual immorality. The Greek word used here is *porneia*, which is a broad term that includes all forms of sex outside marriage: fornication, adultery, incest, prostitution, pornography – every form of sexual practice that is outside of the context of marriage (see 5:31 and Day 38). In the words of John Stott: 'This was a high and holy standard to demand, for immorality was rife in Asia. And since the Greek goddess Artemis, "Diana of the Ephesians", was regarded as a fertility goddess, sexual orgies were regularly associated with her worship'.[1] We could add, it is also a 'high and holy standard' in the Western world of the twenty-first century, where sex and sexual gratification are often raised to the level of worship.

The second warning is against 'impurity', already referred to in 4:19, which is linked to sexual immorality but may have included all forms of 'riotous and excessive living'.[2]

The final warning is against 'greed', which may well be linked to the first two references to sexual sins. Lincoln interprets it as 'unrestrained sexual greed whereby a person assumes that others exist for his or her own gratification'.[3] Similarly, Stott links this to the tenth commandment, where the coveting of a neighbour's wife was specifically prohibited. But while this greed certainly has application in the sexual arena, the scope is also broader: 'It simply refers to the insatiable desire to acquire more and more, whatever the object.'[4] In particular, greed is regularly linked to the dangers of the love of money. Once again, this first-century warning is so applicable to the twenty-first century, where materialism and covetousness dominate so much of our world, particularly in the West.

Why should there not be even a hint of sexual immorality, impurity and greed? Because they are 'improper for God's holy people'. This is our new identity: we are in Christ, God's workmanship, His new creation (2:10), being built together to become a 'holy temple in the Lord' (2:21). We therefore have both the high calling and the 'power' to live free. So let's not let even 'a hint' of these things be in our lives and in our midst!

This challenge will apply to each of us in different ways, but to live free from all forms of sexual immorality and impurity, we have to take a radical stand. We need to decide, before temptation comes, that as God's holy people we will not dishonour our Lord and Saviour by allowing any sin or compromise into our lives. This heart decision means practically that we will need to be wise in terms of what TV we will not watch, what internet sites we will not visit and what relationships we will not allow to become too close. Making oneself accountable to other trusted Christian friends and leaders is normally a good deterrent and is highly recommended.

We have to be similarly radical with the issue of greed, especially in the area of money. There are a number of things we can do to overcome here. First, we need to regularly re-surrender all that we have, giving thanks to the God who gave it to us in the first place, and choosing to live a life of contentment in all circumstances (see Phil. 4:11–13). Allied with contentment, the greatest antidote to greed is generosity. There is much in the Bible on this whole subject. As we saw on Day 19 (see 4:28), one of the main purposes for acquiring wealth is so that we can give to others in need. Elsewhere, we are consistently encouraged to bring our tithe first to God, which helps remind us that He is first and He is our source.

REFLECT AND RESPOND

- **With this in mind, take time to ponder. Are there any areas of sexual immorality, impurity or greed in your life right now? If so, ask for God's forgiveness and make a choice today to turn around and live differently.**

- **If you have struggled for a long time in the area of sexual sin, you may need the help of a mature Christian or church leader who can help you get free and stay free.**

- **Examine how you are doing with regard to greed and covetousness. Spend some time thanking God for all that He has given you, and invite Him to show you how you can grow in being generous.**

MEMORY VERSE

'Be imitators of God, therefore, as dearly loved children and live a life of love, just as Christ loved us and gave himself up for us as a fragrant offering and sacrifice to God.'

EPHESIANS 5:1–2 (NIV 1984)

NO IMPURE TALK

'Nor should there be obscenity, foolish talk or coarse joking, which are out of place, but rather thanksgiving.' **EPHESIANS 5:4**

In his recent autobiography, *So, Anyway...*, the great English comedian and actor John Cleese gave an interesting assessment of the place of swearing in comedy: 'generally, I was opposed to it. My reasons were not puritanical but purist comedic ones. Quite simply, I regarded swearing as a form of cheating, a lazy way of getting a laugh out of material that wasn't intrinsically funny enough.'[1] Cleese is essentially saying there is something base and cheap about bad language. What makes this an even more surprising admission is that it comes from the world of TV comedy, where it is often thought that 'nothing is sacred'.

Here in Ephesians 5:4, Paul warns us against obscenity on much higher grounds than 'purist' comedic ones. Linked to the previous verse, where he emphasises the need to avoid any hint of sexual immorality, impurity and greed (5:3), he proceeds here to highlight the need to shun 'obscenity, foolish talk or coarse joking'. The word 'obscenity' includes the idea of indecent behaviour or wickedness, but in this context it is probably linked to the other two terms, 'foolish talk' and 'coarse joking', and would simply mean disgraceful speech. The second term, 'foolish talk', includes dirty talk of a sexual nature, but should not be seen as limited to this. The third term, 'coarse joking', was most often used positively in Greek literature to mean 'wittiness'. However, it also had negative connotations, to mean 'some kind of inhumane or degrading jesting … often at somebody else's expense'.[2] While Paul is not denigrating the use of humour per se, he is clearly saying that such unholy talk and twisted humour is considered to be 'out of place'; that is, thoroughly inappropriate for God's holy people. One might add that so, too, is sarcasm and gossip. Before you speak, it's worth asking yourself whether you would say what you were about to say, if the person you were going to talk about were standing there with you.

Paul doesn't just warn us of negative actions or speech but encourages us to replace them with something altogether positive: thanksgiving. At first, this might seem a strange contrast. Wouldn't it be better to talk about replacing unholy actions and words with holiness or purity? Yet it may well be that Paul deliberately chooses thanksgiving to highlight the following: 'Whereas sexual impurity and covetousness both express acquisitiveness, thanksgiving is the exact opposite, and so the antidote is required; it is the recognition of God's generosity.'[3] In other words, God is the Creator and the source of everything good, including sex. The God of the Bible doesn't have a low view of sex, but an extremely high view of sex since He created it. It's His idea. Hence, he doesn't want us to cheapen it, or any other of His good gifts, but rather to give thanks for them. As we give thanks for what He has given us in all areas of life, we will not only be glorifying Him, but will be filling our mouths with pure rather than impure language. This emphasis on thanksgiving is a theme that Paul will return to in 5:20, which we will look at in more detail on Day 34.

How are we to live in the light of this exhortation? By recognising that our new identity in Christ requires a new lifestyle, particularly in the area of our speech. We have already seen the importance of changing our words from deceitful to truthful (4:25), from unwholesome to edifying (4:29), and from bitter to loving (4:30–31). Here, Paul adds further detail. We must rid ourselves of all impure talk and replace this with thanksgiving. As Lloyd-Jones helpfully emphasises: 'The Christian is not to be a dull and morbid and an uninteresting person, not for a moment! … He is to express joy and happiness in life, for he is one who has got a profound sense of gratitude to God and to the Lord Jesus Christ within him, and is a man who *wants* to be giving thanks!'⁴

REFLECT AND RESPOND

- **Are you prone to sarcasm, coarse jokes or gossip? Invite the Lord to shine His light into your life. Ask Him to help you change your speech so that it builds up and honours others.**

- **If you live or work in a culture where 'foolish talk or coarse joking' are the norm, consider what steps you need to take to bring life to that culture. Determine to be someone who actively encourages and speaks well of others, and ask the Holy Spirit for His anointing to bring His peace and presence through your words.**

MEMORY VERSE

'Be imitators of God, therefore, as dearly loved children and live a life of love, just as Christ loved us and gave himself up for us as a fragrant offering and sacrifice to God.'

EPHESIANS 5:1–2 (NIV 1984)

DAY 25

JUDGMENT FOR DISOBEDIENCE

'For of this you can be sure: no immoral, impure or greedy person – such a person is an idolater – has any inheritance in the kingdom of Christ and of God. Let no one deceive you with empty words, for because of such things God's wrath comes on those who are disobedient. Therefore do not be partners with them.' **EPHESIANS 5:5–7**

Good parents will sometimes need to warn their little children of the dangerous consequences of foolish actions. Whether it be care in crossing a busy road, staying away from a fire, swimming close to the shore in the sea, parents who love their children will strongly urge them to be careful.

Here, the Holy Spirit is doing just that through Paul. In 5:3–4, Paul has urged Christians not to be involved in sexual immorality, impurity greed or obscene talk. Now in 5:5–7 he reinforces this with stark warnings concerning the consequences for those who live this way. In case we were in any doubt as to the importance of what he is about to say, he starts by using this phrase: 'For of this you can be sure'. He is drawing attention to a certainty – that those who habitually practise the sins of 5:3–4 will be excluded from God's kingdom.

It is vital that we note that the emphasis has shifted away from sinful practices in 5:3–4 to the people themselves: 'no immoral, impure or greedy *person*' (my emphasis). The clear implication is that this is not a warning of judgment for Christians who may, through weakness, occasionally fall into sin – and in repentance, ask for forgiveness and the strength to be faithful. We can be confident that this is not the case, since Paul has already gone to such great lengths to assure his hearers that they have a secure hope of inheriting their glorious future in Christ (see 1:13–14,18; 4:4,30). But these verses are nevertheless a solemn warning against a persistent lifestyle of sin.

In effect, Paul is urging Christians not to live like unbelievers whose life and lifestyle is characterised by immorality, impurity and idolatry. This link to idolatry is a significant one. In the words of Peter O'Brien: 'Along with greed for riches and power, sexual lust is an idolatrous obsession; it places self-gratification or another person at the centre of one's existence, and thus is the worship of the creature rather than the Creator'.[1]

The solemn warning here is that such self-centred idolaters have no inheritance in 'the kingdom of Christ and of God'. What does this mean? It seems as if Paul is making a distinction between the present reign of the kingdom (of Christ), and its future aspect (of God). But since Christ and God (the Father) are One, it is also true that 'One and the same kingdom belongs to, and is ruled by Christ and God. Let the readers, then, heed Paul's exhortations. Those in slavery to their sexual appetites are surely excluded from the rule of Christ and God.'[2]

Paul then goes on to strongly encourage Christians not to listen to contrary advice: 'let no one deceive you with empty words'. Who these deceiving influences were is not specified. It could be fellow Christians or Christian teachers who emphasise a libertarian lifestyle, or 'cheap grace'. But it seems more likely from the context overall that these were unbelieving Gentiles – in other words, people from the surrounding culture. The reason these false words are 'empty' is because of the sobering reality that because of such sinful practices

'God's wrath' is coming. God's wrath is His steady righteous anger against 'those who are disobedient' and may relate to present-day wrath, but more likely is pointing the way to the future judgment in the age to come. Again, it's important to emphasise that the reference to 'the disobedient' points 'not to those who commit the occasional act of disobedience but to men and women whose lives are characterised by disobedience'.[3]

So, what does it mean practically not to be 'partners' with such people? Clearly this doesn't mean that we are to make ourselves absent from the world, or from those who are living lives and practising lifestyles that are ungodly. (Jesus here is our model, in that He prioritised time with 'sinners'.) Rather, it means that we are not to partner with or participate in practices that are clearly unholy.

All of this doesn't mean that we should succumb to an unhealthy fear of judgment – since we have already been 'sealed for the day of redemption' (4:30) – but it does mean that the call to live holy lives is a serious one. The God of grace, and this wonderful epistle of grace, in no way condones sin. Rather, God calls us and empowers us to a radically new life in Christ.

REFLECT AND RESPOND

- **Pray today for the people in your life who haven't yet met Jesus and haven't come to understand the amazing life of freedom He offers. Pray that they would come to know Him and accept Him as their Saviour, receiving His grace and forgiveness.**

- **Pray for yourself and your family; that you would be empowered by the Holy Spirit to live a pure and holy life that is pleasing to the Lord.**

MEMORY VERSE

'Be imitators of God, therefore, as dearly loved children and live a life of love, just as Christ loved us and gave himself up for us as a fragrant offering and sacrifice to God.'

EPHESIANS 5:1–2 (NIV 1984)

DAY 26

LIVE IN THE LIGHT

'For you were once darkness, but now you are light in the Lord. Live as children of light (for the fruit of the light consists in all goodness, righteousness and truth) and find out what pleases the Lord.' **EPHESIANS 5:8–10**

I heard about a story of a young police officer who was taking his final exam at Hendon Police College in North London. The first three questions in this exam were relatively easy. And then he got to question four, which went like this: 'You're on patrol in outer London when an explosion occurs in a gas main in a nearby street. On investigation, you find that a large hole has been blown in the footpath and that there is an overturned van lying nearby. Inside the van there's a strong smell of alcohol. Both occupants, a man and a woman, are injured. You recognise the woman as the wife of your Divisional Inspector, who is away on a course. A passing motorist stops to offer you assistance, but you realise that he is a man who's wanted for armed robbery. Suddenly another man runs out of a nearby house, shouting that his wife is expecting a baby and the shock of the explosion has made the birth imminent. Another man is crying for help, having been blown into an adjacent canal by the explosion, and he cannot swim. Bearing in mind the provisions of the Mental Health Act, describe in a few words what actions you would take.' The police officer thought for a moment, picked up his pen and wrote: 'I would take off my uniform and mingle with the crowd.'

We can be tempted to think like that – to take off our Christian uniform and mingle with the crowd, to be like everybody else, because it's so much easier. But what we're called to be is distinctive – to retain our Christian identity wherever we are, whatever the circumstance.

Here Paul emphasises this in the strongest possible way by introducing a new image of the transformed life: 'you were once darkness, now you are light in the Lord. Live as children of light … and find out what pleases the Lord.' Notice that he doesn't just say that Christians are those who used to live in darkness and are now living in the light, although that would be true. Rather, he is saying something even more wonderful and fundamental: you 'were' darkness, 'now you *are* light in the Lord' (my emphasis). In other words the transformation is not just environmental, but internal. It is *we* who have changed, so much so that we are now light, by virtue of our new identity in Christ. This new picture of the contrast between darkness and light continues through to 5:14, and once again serves as the basis for why and how we can live differently.

This is Paul's primary way of motivating us as Christians: know your new identity in Christ, then live in the 'light' of that new identity! If, through the work of God in Christ, we are now light, then it is obvious for us to 'live as children of light'. This means that our whole lives and lifestyle should be characterised by everything that comes from being in relationship with the God who is light, and being saved by Jesus who is the light of the world, and our being 'in' Him.

So what does living as children of light look like? It will be a life of 'goodness, righteousness and truth'. Goodness is something that flows from the God who is good, and is a fruit of the Spirit (see Gal. 5:22–23). Good works are something that those who are newly recreated in Christ are now to practise (Eph. 2:10). Righteousness and truth are also both characteristics of God, and, as we have seen previously (see 4:25), are very much qualities of the new life in Christ.

The practical outworking of living as children of light is that in all situations we are to 'find out what pleases the Lord'. Whereas previously our 'dark' lives were focused on pleasing ourselves, now as those who are in the light we are to find out what pleases God. We do this by looking at the truth that is in Christ (4:22), by following the instructions in His Word (4:25–29), and by obeying the promptings of the Spirit and not grieving Him (4:30).

REFLECT AND RESPOND

- **You are light! Whether you feel like it today or not, if you are in Christ then you are by your new identity 'light in the Lord'. Meditate on this truth and let it impact your thoughts and actions today.**

- **Determine to be someone who always seeks to know what pleases the Lord and to understand His heart.**

MEMORY VERSE

'Be imitators of God, therefore, as dearly loved children and live a life of love, just as Christ loved us and gave himself up for us as a fragrant offering and sacrifice to God.'

EPHESIANS 5:1–2 (NIV 1984)

SHUN THE DARKNESS AND SHINE!

'Have nothing to do with the fruitless deeds of darkness, but rather expose them. It is shameful even to mention what the disobedient do in secret. But everything exposed by the light becomes visible – and everything that is illuminated becomes a light.'
EPHESIANS 5:11–13

I don't know whether you've ever had this experience. You've taken a bright torch and shone it into a dark area that hasn't seen the light for a long while, such as a cellar. As the light shines it exposes lots of things that have been hidden – cobwebs, dust and even some creatures! The light exposes and illuminates the things hidden in darkness.

Paul here is continuing his theme that believers who are 'light in the Lord' should live as children of light (5:8–10).They must now separate themselves from all 'fruitless deeds of darkness'. The fact that these deeds are seen as 'shameful' and performed 'in secret' suggests that he may well be referring yet again to sexual immorality, but also possibly occult ('hidden') activity.

Yet the emphasis here is not just on shunning the darkness but rather fulfilling our call to shine the light and thereby 'expose' these deeds and make everything 'visible'. There is some debate as to what this is referring to. Some have suggested that this is a call for believers to confront fellow believers but the overall context of the whole passage is the contrast between believers in Christ and the unbelieving world. Hence, the 'exposing' of the 'fruitless deeds of darkness' concerns the lives of unbelievers. So, what can this mean and how does it apply? It surely doesn't mean that we go on a judgmental finger-pointing campaign of 'sinners' as the Pharisees did. Rather, we should look to Jesus, who was a 'friend of sinners', and who through His light attracted people to Him, exposing their sin and offering them a better way. Similarly, Paul in his ministry, including notably in Ephesus in Acts 19, exposed and transformed the lives of many. Now that we are 'light in the Lord' we, too, can shine with the light of Christ, thereby exposing and potentially transforming the lives of those around us. In the words of Martyn Lloyd-Jones: 'Our business is to let them know about the change that has come to us. We are to give them glimpses of a better life, a purer and a cleaner life, yes, and a life which is much more enjoyable … Holiness ought to be attractive, it ought to be loving, it ought to be enticing, it ought to be charming, it ought to draw people … We are to remove the unfruitful works of darkness by being light, by being what we are, in our conversation, in our speech, in our exposition of the gospel.'[1]

Throughout church history we have seen the power of an individual or a community who lived as children of light. One such light bearer was the American revivalist preacher Charles Finney, who saw remarkable outpourings of the Holy Spirit during his ministry, especially between 1820 and 1830. Sometimes the power of God was so strong in Finney's meetings that almost entire audiences fell on their knees in prayer, or were prostrated on the floor, overwhelmed by the convicting power of the Holy Spirit. It has been reported that in several major cities in the state of New York, when Finney was holding meetings – cities like Syracuse, Rochester, Utica, Albany – a holy power would seem to settle upon the entire city. On several occasions it was reported that the conviction power of the Holy Spirit so poured through Finney that people were brought under conviction just by his presence. One notable example reportedly took place during Finney's visit to a cotton mill near the village of Whitesboro, about three miles west of Utica. He first had an encounter with a woman who came under conviction while making a rude comment with a fellow worker. Mr Finney approached her and spoke with her. She soon showed a deep sense of sin. The feeling spread through the establishment like fire, and in a few hours almost every person employed there was under conviction. The feeling was so pervasive that the owner, though a worldly man, was astounded and stopped all work to hold a prayer meeting. In a few days, the owner and nearly all the employees (about 3,000 people) were fully converted.[2]

REFLECT AND RESPOND

- **May Charles Finney's life inspire and encourage you today to live as a child of the light.**

- **Pray for God to move in revival power once again in the nations; that His light would shine bringing conviction and transformation to many.**

MEMORY VERSE

'Be imitators of God, therefore, as dearly loved children and live a life of love, just as Christ loved us and gave himself up for us as a fragrant offering and sacrifice to God.'
EPHESIANS 5:1–2 (NIV 1984)

DAY 28

TIME TO WAKE UP!

'This is why it is said: "Wake up, sleeper,
rise from the dead, and Christ will shine on you."'
EPHESIANS 5:14

I don't know what you are like at waking up. Being a naturally early riser, I tend to wake up and want to get up fairly soon. However, there are times during the day when I feel a bit sleepy and need to 'wake up' again in order to function at my best. I find that a brisk walk in the fresh air, sometimes combined with some caffeine, normally does the trick! My wife, Karen, who generally sleeps better than I do, and is less of a 'lark', normally needs a cup of tea in bed before feeling fully physically awake!

To fully wake up and stay awake physically is very important. To fully wake up and stay alert spiritually is *all*-important. That is why here in Ephesians 5:14 Paul issues a spiritual wake up call. The introductory phrase 'this is why it is said' has occasioned much debate amongst commentators. Many argue that this is a fragment from a baptismal hymn, reminding the Ephesians of the summons and promise they have received at their baptism: having been once dead (asleep), they are now raised up to life (have been awoken). Others, such as O'Brien, rightly point out that baptism is not specifically referred to here, and suggest that it is more likely to be a reference to conversion, and may be based on Old Testament scriptures such as Isaiah 26:19 and 60:1–3.

If this is the context, then how does it apply? First, it's a clear wake up call to those who are already Christians. If we assume Isaiah 60:1 as a backdrop ('Arise, shine, for your light has come, and the glory of the LORD rises upon you') and understand this verse (Eph. 5:14) in the context of the preceding passage (Eph. 5:8–13), it seems that this has a dual application for our lives. It's both a reminder of what God has already done in Christ in transforming us from darkness into light, as well as a call for us to live differently by shunning all works of darkness and living as children of light. The promise is that Christ has shone on us and will shine upon us as we continue to live in the light.

Secondly, there is the promise of an overflow into the lives of those who are not yet Christians. Isaiah 60:2–3 emphasises the 'darkness' and 'thick darkness' that covers the unbelieving world, but there is the promise that as the glory of the Lord shines on His people, 'Nations will come to your light, and kings to the brightness of your dawn'. This links to what we saw yesterday in Ephesians 5:13 and how the promise is that as we who are light live as children of light, so the light of Christ will shine on unbelievers, exposing and potentially transforming their lives, too.

This is the urgent need in our world today. We need a sovereign outpouring of God's Spirit to bring revival and awakening. Revival by definition refers to something that was once alive and needs to be revived; so it is primarily for believers and the Church. Awakening refers to those who are asleep, and refers primarily to unbelievers and a lost world. In practice, when there is a true revival, Christians and the Christian Church come alive again, and the result can be an awakening of a lost world.

One of the greatest revivals and awakenings took place in the eighteenth century under the leadership of men like George Whitefield and John Wesley. It started in the 1730s with men who, like themselves, gathered in religious societies. As many got converted and others were 'revived' in their faith, the emboldened Whitefield and Wesley began to take the good news out beyond the societies and outside of the churches, preaching to the thousands in the open air. On one such occasion, Whitefield took the light of the gospel out to the Kingswood colliers, just outside Bristol. This was his report: 'The first discovery of their being affected was to see the white gutters made by their tears which plentifully fell down their black cheeks, as they came out of their coal pits. Hundreds and hundreds of them were soon brought under deep convictions, which, as the event proved, happily ended in a sound and thorough conversion. The change was visible to all…'[1] Whitefield himself then travelled to America and was able to unite a growing revival movement across the colonies, before going to Scotland in 1741–1742, where he saw a similar response. The breadth and depth of this outpouring was such that many historians have called it the Great Awakening. My earnest prayer is that God would bring another revival and an even greater awakening in our time and in our world.

REFLECT AND RESPOND

- **At the end of this week, take some time to pray for revival for the Christian Church globally. Pray for an awakening in our nations; that Jesus' light would shine and that multitudes would come to know Him as their Lord and Saviour.**

- **Thank God for every church in your community. Pray that they would be empowered by the Holy Spirit to fulfil their purpose and further God's kingdom.**

MEMORY VERSE

'Be imitators of God, therefore, as dearly loved children and live a life of love, just as Christ loved us and gave himself up for us as a fragrant offering and sacrifice to God.'

EPHESIANS 5:1–2 (NIV 1984)

WEEK 5

LIVE IN WISDOM AND BY THE SPIRIT

'Be very careful, then, how you live – not as unwise but as wise, making the most of every opportunity, because the days are evil. Therefore do not be foolish, but understand what the Lord's will is. Do not get drunk on wine, which leads to debauchery. Instead, be filled with the Spirit, speaking to one another with psalms, hymns, and songs from the Spirit. Sing and make music from your heart to the Lord, always giving thanks to God the Father for everything, in the name of our Lord Jesus Christ. Submit to one another out of reverence for Christ.'

EPHESIANS 5:15–21

DAY 29

BE CAREFUL AND WISE

'Be very careful, then, how you live – not as unwise but as wise' **EPHESIANS 5:15**

If you could ask for one thing from God, what would it be? More money, better health, fame, improved relationships, success at work? In the Old Testament we see an occasion when God appeared to King Solomon in a dream and told him he could ask for anything and it would be given him. Solomon asked for one thing: wisdom. So God gave him wisdom and also what he hadn't asked for – wealth and honour. In fact, so great was Solomon's wisdom that he was the wisest man of his day, and for a season he also became hugely wealthy and successful. Sadly, Solomon stopped being wise, and started acting foolishly, with disastrous consequences.

As Paul here refers to the contrast between the unwise and the wise, he is drawing on a rich tradition of Old Testament wisdom literature which predates and includes the time of Solomon. In key texts such as Psalm 1 and Proverbs 4, there is a clear call to walk on the path of wisdom, alongside warnings against walking on the path of wickedness and folly. In fact, wisdom is something that is to be cherished above all else: 'The beginning of wisdom is this: get wisdom. Though it cost all you have, get understanding. Cherish her, and she will exalt you; embrace her, and she will honour you' (Prov. 4:7–8). Paul would echo this clear call.

Here in Ephesians 5:15, he starts a new section by emphasising the importance of shunning folly and living in wisdom, especially the need to be 'very careful' concerning the way we live our lives. His use of the word 'live' (literally 'walk') links this exhortation back to the previous section in 4:1–5:14, where the word has already been used five times to emphasise a new life and new lifestyle. As he has contrasted the need to take great care to leave the old life and live in the new (4:17–5:2), and to shun the darkness and shine as lights (5:8–14), so he now urges us to be very careful not to live a life of folly but of wisdom: 'not as unwise, but as wise'.

So what then is the wisdom that the Bible generally, and Paul here, is referring to? It is not the same as knowledge, but rather is the power and ability to *apply* knowledge. In the words of Lloyd-Jones, 'it is the faculty for making use of your intelligence and knowledge and for bringing it into relationship with the ordinary, practical daily things of life'.[1] It is vital that we each grow in this kind of practical wisdom.

But it is also important, in the light of Ephesians and the Bible in general, that we understand that this wisdom is founded upon a right 'fear' (or reverence) of the Lord and is centred on Christ Himself, in whom are hidden all the treasures of wisdom and understanding (Col. 2:3). It is connected very strongly to walking in a God-centred, Christ-exalting way, and concerns the ability to practically apply knowledge to our daily lives, so that we live life in a way that pleases God (see more on Day 31).

REFLECT AND RESPOND

- **Given the importance of wisdom and the call to walk 'not as unwise but as wise', take some time now to pray. Repent of areas where you know you are living your life in 'folly', without having God at the centre.**

- **Ask God for wisdom. As you do, be encouraged by this promise: 'If any of you lacks wisdom, he should ask God, who gives generously to all without finding fault, and it will be given to him' (James 1:5).**

MEMORY VERSE

'Be very careful, then, how you live – not as unwise but as wise'
EPHESIANS 5:15

SEIZE THE DAY

'making the most of every opportunity, because the days are evil.' **EPHESIANS 5:16**

Imagine there is a bank account that credits your account each morning with £86,400. It carries over no balance from day to day. Every evening the bank deletes whatever part of the balance you failed to use during the day. What would you do? Draw out every penny?

Each of us has such a bank and its name is 'time'. Every morning, it credits us each with 86,400 seconds. Every night it writes off as a loss whatever of this you failed to invest to a good purpose. It carries over no balance. It allows no overdraft. Each day it opens a new account for you. Each night it burns the remains of the day. If you fail to use the day's deposits, the loss is yours. There is no drawing against tomorrow. You must live in the present on today's deposits. Invest in it so as to get from it the utmost in health and happiness. The clock is running. Make the most of today!

Here in 5:16, Paul follows up on his general call to walk carefully and wisely (5:15) with a specific exhortation to be wise in the use of time. The phrase literally reads 'redeeming the time' or 'buying back time', but the NIV here conveys the general metaphorical meaning correctly as 'making the most of every opportunity'. In the words of one commentator: 'Believers will act wisely by snapping up every opportunity that comes'.[1]

The reason given here for making the most of every opportunity is 'because the days are evil'. As well as a general description of evil in the world, Paul is using a classic Old Testament and Jewish understanding of the difference between 'the present evil age' (Gal. 1:4; Eph. 6:13) and 'the coming age' of salvation. The present age that we live in is in some measure under the control of the evil one, who keeps those outside of Christ in bondage (2:1–3). But there is good news for those who are in Christ: 'the Ephesian Christians have already participated in the world to come, the powers of the new age have broken in upon them, and they have become "light in the Lord"'[2] (5:8). This means that they, and we, are not to fear these days, but to live carefully and diligently, making the most of every opportunity, living as light in the darkness and using every occasion for doing good.

This doesn't mean that we are to live frantically or become even more hurried than we already are! If we look at the life of Jesus, He doesn't come across as being rushed. It's also important for us to grasp that Scripture has a positive attitude to rest, most notably through the principle of the Sabbath – taking one day in seven to rest. In fact, when we properly rest, we can then work more effectively and productively.

So, if making the most of every opportunity isn't about living more frantically, what does it mean for us? It involves viewing our whole lives, including our time, as a gift from God, and that we are to use our time as good stewards, living from God-given priorities rather than just living from pressure. It includes making sure that we spend time on what really matters: time with the Lord in our personal devotions, time with family and friends, time being with and serving those in our church, time for exercise and relaxation, as well as an appropriate amount of focused time in productive activity or employment.

REFLECT AND RESPOND

- Why not take some time out to make sure that you are using your time in the best way possible? Start by prioritising time with the Lord.

- Consider whether you are using your time most effectively in serving the purpose of God at work, and in and through your church (see Week 2, Eph. 4:7–16).

- Are you taking the opportunities to share the good news of the 'light' of the gospel with those who are not yet Christians?

- Where are you perhaps 'wasting' time? How can you redeem or reclaim this time for good?

MEMORY VERSE

'Be very careful, then, how you live – not as unwise but as wise'
EPHESIANS 5:15

DAY 31

UNDERSTAND
THE LORD'S WILL

'Therefore do not be foolish, but understand what the Lord's will is.' **EPHESIANS 5:17**

Mizuho Securities, a trading company, wanted to sell one share in a company for around 610,000 yen. Sadly, the trader muddled the instruction and made 610,000 shares available for sale for the cost of one yen each. The company did not even have this huge amount of shares available; nevertheless, the stock exchange proceeded with the sale despite protests and it cost the company around 40.7 billion yen. One act of folly can be very costly. Far more costly is to live a *life* of folly.

Here in 5:17, Paul, returning to the theme of folly and wisdom (5:15), first highlights the need to shun a life of folly: 'Therefore do not be foolish'. The word 'foolish' appears 74 times in the Septuagint (the Greek translation of the Old Testament) version of Proverbs to contrast 'the fool' with the one who walks in the way of wisdom. In Proverbs fools are described as those who are lazy (24:30); have uncontrolled tongues (18:6–7); lie (6:12), slander (10:18), quarrel (20:3), and are quick-tempered (14:29); they are proud (13:16); hate knowledge (1:22), despise advice or correction (12:1); and are reckless and careless (14:16). As C.E. Arnold correctly summarises: 'Much of this list corresponds with the kind of moral exhortation Paul has given in Eph. 4:25–5:14'.[1]

Having dealt with the negative call to not be foolish, Paul moves on to a positive call to embrace a life of wisdom, specifically here: 'but understand what the Lord's will is'. It's worth noting from the outset that this is not a verse primarily about getting God's guidance in the specifics of a particular situation – although that of course is important and necessary. Rather, in the context of the moral and ethical exhortation of the previous passage, this most likely refers to the overall need to walk in a way that pleases God – living a new life of purity, love and light. Again, this picks up on Old Testament wisdom literature, where the 'fear of the Lord', that is the right reverence for God, is 'the beginning of wisdom'. After a fruitless search for fulfilment the author of Ecclesiastes concludes that life outside of God and His ways is all 'meaningless' (Eccl. 12:8). His summary is clear: 'here is the conclusion of the matter: fear God and keep his commandments, for this is the duty of all mankind' (Eccl. 12:13).

This Old Testament reference to God's commandments highlights one of the main ways that we understand the Lord's will, which is through His Word. In Psalm 1, for example, the Psalmist highlights that the 'blessed' person will not follow in the path of wickedness (v1). Rather, he or she will 'delight in the law of the Lord', and 'meditate' on the Word 'day and night' in order to be careful to do everything written in it (v2). This word 'meditate' literally means to mutter or murmur. It conveys the idea of getting the Word (here, the Old Testament 'Law' or 'Torah') in our minds, on our hearts and then on our lips, so that we can mutter it throughout the course of our day, and live in the light of its truth.

This is why the fact that you are doing this study is so important! Now, in the New Testament era, we have the fuller revelation of God's purpose for our lives in and through Christ, nowhere more so than in this wonderful letter to the Ephesians. Hence, for those of you who have read (or will read) *Transformed Life*, you will grow in knowing your true identity, place of belonging and purpose in Christ, as you delight in and meditate upon the glorious truths of Ephesians 1–3. Similarly, as we are going through *Transformed Living* and taking time to pause, reflect and meditate on Ephesians 4–6, on how we are to live out our new life in Christ, we will find that we are understanding and living in such a way that 'pleases the Lord'.

The second primary way that we can understand the Lord's will is through the Spirit. Just as we needed the Spirit's help to understand how much God has blessed us in Christ (see 1:17), so now here in 5:17 it is significant that the call to 'understand what the Lord's will is', is followed by the exhortation to 'be filled with the Spirit' (v18), which we will focus on tomorrow. Put simply, we need the Spirit working with the Word to help us understand who we now are in Christ and how we are to live in Him.

So, if once again we are being called to leave a life of folly and live a life of wisdom, understanding the Lord's will, we must embrace a lifestyle that centres on His Word and His Spirit. We need to regularly and daily set aside time to meditate on His Word, allowing the Spirit to illuminate the truths to our hearts and minds, and to remind us and guide us throughout the blessings and challenges of our daily lives.

REFLECT AND RESPOND

- **What would it look like for you to embrace a lifestyle that centres around God's Word and His Spirit?**

- **Thank God that He chooses to illuminate the truth to our hearts and minds, and guides us throughout the blessings and challenges of our daily lives.**

MEMORY VERSE

'Be very careful, then, how you live – not as unwise but as wise'
EPHESIANS 5:15

BE FILLED WITH THE SPIRIT

'Do not get drunk on wine, which leads to debauchery. Instead, be filled with the Spirit'
EPHESIANS 5:18

Every year in this country around 150,000 motorists put the wrong type of fuel into their car, the consequences of which can be very damaging. If you realise early and don't drive the wrongly fuelled car it can be drained for around £100–£200. If you drive it with the wrong fuel for a while it can be even more damaging and expensive to fix. One lady lent her Porsche to a friend who thought he would thank her by filling the car up with petrol. On driving her newly returned 'diesel' car she noticed the problem and drove the chugging vehicle to her garage to be faced with a £14,600 repair bill. The moral of the tale: use the right fuel. And we could add: don't run out of fuel, but keep the car filled up!

If this is true with an inanimate object like a car, how much more with our lives. First, notice the warning on filling ourselves with the wrong substance: 'Do not get drunk on wine, which leads to debauchery'. Some have seen this as a case-specific rebuke against drunkenness at the Lord's Table, similar to that at Corinth (1 Cor. 11:21). The problem is that there is no suggestion from the text itself that this was the case. Others have suggested that there is a reference here to the pagan mystery cult celebrations, especially the cult of Dionysius, the god of wine. But the most convincing interpretation is found in the whole context of 4:17–5:21 where the contrast is between life before and after Christ, as characterised by darkness and light, and by foolishness and wisdom. In this sense, drunkenness is part of living in darkness and folly, whereas being filled with the Spirit is living in light and wisdom. While this is not a Scripture against the use of all alcohol, it is clearly a warning against drinking too much since this leads to a loss of self-control and a greater proneness to a life of impurity and folly.

Then to the positive: 'Instead, be filled with the Spirit'. This reference to the Spirit is not an isolated one. Rather, Paul's writings in general, and Ephesians in particular, abound with 'Spirit' texts. In Ephesians 1–3, the Holy Spirit plays a central role in us being 'in Christ' both individually and as the people of God (1:3,13–14,17; 2:18,20–22; 3:16). In the light of this it is not surprising that we are then exhorted to keep the unity of the 'one Spirit' (4:3–4), and are warned not to 'grieve the Holy Spirit of God' (4:30). Here, in a kind of summary and climactic statement about the role of the Spirit and indeed of our call to live the new life of holiness, love, light and wisdom (4:17–5:17), Paul makes a central exhortation: 'be filled with the Spirit', both for corporate worship (5:18–19), and in order to maintain the unity of the Spirit, particularly within the household (5:21–33). Even our warfare is to be conducted with the Spirit's help, specifically by using the sword of the Spirit and by praying in the Spirit (6:17–18). Here in (5:18), the call is to be filled with the Spirit. It is crucial to realise that the tense used here is the present continuous, and could be translated 'go on being filled with the Spirit'. Nothing could be more important for the believers then and for us now. We don't just need to receive the Spirit at conversion and be initially filled with the Spirit (see Acts 2:4,38–39; 19:1–8). Rather, we need to be *continually filled* with the Spirit. This is hugely important. Just as you can damage your car engine by running on empty, even more so we will 'damage' our lives if we try and live without being continually filled with the Spirit, who is of course not an inanimate substance, but the third Person of the Trinity, the very empowering presence of God.

So, what does it mean to be continually filled with the Spirit? Some have seen a deliberate contrast between being 'drunk' on wine and being 'drunk' in the Spirit, similar to the outsiders' view of the disciples in Acts 2:13. In this regard, the contrast could be between two states: 'that of intoxication and that of inspiration'.[1] However, here in Ephesians 5:18 it is much more likely that Paul is highlighting that we need the Spirit's empowering to help us live the new life (see 4:17–5:17), which will in turn affect every area of our worship and relationships (5:19–6:9). Put simply, we must be ever filled with the Spirit. This is not a luxury for an 'enthusiastic' minority: it's a necessity for all of those who are in Christ.

REFLECT AND RESPOND

- **If you are a Christian, then the Holy Spirit is living in you! How well do you feel you are hosting Him?**

- **Thank God that He chooses to live in you by His Spirit and ask Him to keep filling you up to overflowing so that you can live a life that enriches others.**

MEMORY VERSE

'Be very careful, then, how you live – not as unwise but as wise'
EPHESIANS 5:15

DAY 33

LIVE A LIFE OF PRAISE

'speaking to one another with psalms, hymns, and songs from the Spirit. Sing and make music from your heart to the Lord' **EPHESIANS 5:19**

It's probably due to years of misspent youth on the football terraces at Maine Road, Manchester, but I have long been convinced of the power of singing. Our singing as fans functioned on a number of levels. Firstly, it was an expression of support and loyalty, even when the team was doing very badly. Secondly, it was a way of expressing appreciation when the team was winning, playing well, or had just scored. But thirdly, the very fact of us singing seemed to change the atmosphere itself, often spurring on the team to play much better.

When I became a Christian and started worshipping in church services, it was no surprise to me that I found a similar, but far greater dynamic as I joined in sung praises to the only One who is truly worthy. It seemed wholly appropriate to worship God out of love and loyalty to Him for His holiness and grace. It was entirely apt to praise Him for the mighty deeds that He had done. Moreover, as we drew near to Him in praise and worship, there was often a tangible change in the atmosphere as He responded by coming with His manifest presence, thus enabling *us* to do better!

Here in 5:19, Paul highlights that one of the great hallmarks of living the new Spirit-filled life in Christ is speaking to one another in 'psalms, hymns, and songs from the Spirit'. It is important to note the strong connection between the Spirit and worship: both from the previous verse 'be filled with the Spirit' (5:18) and the reference here to 'songs from the Spirit'. So what is the link between the two? Most commentators have assumed that the call to 'speak' and 'sing' (v19) is the *result* of being filled with the Spirit. Certainly, there is scriptural warrant for this approach, with Jesus Himself highlighting that 'the mouth speaks what the heart is full of' (Matt. 12:34). Moreover, this would fit with later references to the Spirit in this letter, where the speaking of the Word of God and the speaking to God in prayer are both results of being inspired by the Spirit (6:17–18). C.E. Arnold has, however, suggested another interpretation, which is that worship is the *means* by which we can be filled with the Spirit. He adds: 'this is not a mechanistic approach, but rather a recognition that God meets his people and strengthens them by his Spirit as they corporately worship him and praise his name'.[1] Certainly this has scriptural support both from the Old Testament (2 Chron. 5:13–14) and New Testament (Acts 13:2). So which interpretation is correct? The evidence from the order of the Ephesians 5:18–19 text suggests that the primary meaning is that worship is a primary result or 'overflow' of being filled with the Spirit. However, the other suggestion, that worship is also a means by which we are filled with the Spirit, is also true both scripturally and experientially.

As to the nature of this Spirit-filled worship, it is both horizontal and vertical. Today we are focusing on the horizontal (5:19), tomorrow on the vertical (5:19–20). The horizontal aspect of our worship is encapsulated in the phrase, 'speak to one another'. In the parallel text in Colossians the purpose of this horizontal worship is 'to teach and admonish one another' (3:16). Here in Ephesians 5:19, it just says 'speak', but it seems likely that instruction and edification are in mind (see 4:30).

The three categories of 'psalms, hymns, and songs from the Spirit' are clearly linked but probably each have their distinct focus. The 'psalms' may well be referring to the Psalms of the Old Testament (see Luke 20:42; 24:44), which would have been the hymn book of the day, but also may be a more general term meaning a song of praise (see 1 Cor. 14:26). The word 'hymns' in the Greek world was used exclusively of songs sung to deities or heroes, and so would be the singing of praise to or about God, and now about Christ, as the evidence from the book of Revelation makes especially clear (Rev. 4:11; 5:9). The 'songs from the Spirit' relates back to the Spirit and can mean broadly 'Spirit-inspired'. In the view of Gordon Fee, based on the evidence of 1 Corinthians 14:15–16 and 26, 'this most likely indicates a kind of charismatic hymnody in which Spirit-inspired and therefore often spontaneous, songs were offered in the context of congregational worship'.[2] Whereas Peter O'Brien points out: 'That such hymns can be described as "spiritual" says nothing about their spontaneity; instead, the focus is on the source of their inspiration, namely, the Holy Spirit'.[3]

Whatever the precise meanings of 'psalms, hymns, and songs from the Spirit', Paul's point is clear. We are not to be drunk with wine (and sing drunken songs), but we are to be filled with the Spirit and speak to one another in the context of worship. Not only is the Spirit the source of our worship, but He moves and refills us in the context of worship.

REFLECT AND RESPOND

- **Set aside some time this week to read from the book of Psalms. Take heart from the psalmists, who wrote and sang praise amidst the greatest joys and challenges of life.**

- **Thank God for the privilege of worship. Determine to continue seeking His presence, both in corporate and private times of worship.**

MEMORY VERSE

'Be very careful, then, how you live – not as unwise but as wise'
EPHESIANS 5:15

LIVE A LIFE OF THANKSGIVING

'Sing and make music from your heart to the Lord, always giving thanks to God the Father for everything, in the name of our Lord Jesus Christ.'
EPHESIANS 5:19–20

In her wonderful book, *The Hiding Place*, Corrie Ten Boom talks about the harrowing experience she and her sister Betsie suffered of being held in a Nazi concentration camp. They had managed to smuggle a Bible into the camp, an amazing feat in itself, but what seemed just as incredible was the fact that the guards never entered their barracks. This meant they were able to hold Bible studies and prayer meetings together, which saw many women in their barracks come to faith in Jesus. In one Bible study, Corrie's sister Betsie came to the conclusion that in all things they must be thankful. Not surprisingly, Corrie found this to be quite a challenge as a prisoner in a flea-infested concentration camp, especially as Betsie wanted her to be thankful for the fleas themselves! Even this was to change as Corrie explains, 'One day, Betsie grabbed my arm and whispered, "I know why no one has bothered our Bible studies. I overheard some of the guards talking. None of them wants to come into Barracks 28 *because of the fleas*!" I wanted to laugh. "All right, Lord. Thank you for the fleas!"'[1]

Indeed, one of the hallmarks of the new life in Christ is a life of thanksgiving, expressed here in Ephesians 5:20, 'always giving thanks to God the Father for everything'. Preceding the call to thanksgiving is the exhortation to 'Sing and make music from your heart to the Lord'. This vertical call to worship is linked to the previous verses, with the emphasis on 'be filled with the Spirit' (5:18) and the horizontal call to speak 'to one another with psalms, hymns, and songs from the Spirit'. The call to worship 'from your heart' is not just a reference to one's emotions, although it includes that. 'Rather, *heart* here signifies the whole of one's being. The entire person should be filled with songs of praise, thereby expressing the reality of life in the Spirit.'[2]

Notice, too, that true worship involves all three Persons of the Trinity: it must be inspired by the Spirit (5:18–19), be directed 'to the Lord' and done 'in the name of our Lord Jesus Christ' (5:20), ultimately ascending in thanks 'to God the Father'. The fact that the singing and making music is to the Lord, clearly a reference to Jesus, is remarkable (the parallel passage in Col. 3:16 is to 'God'). This focus on the praise of Christ in early Christian worship did not escape the notice of Pliny, the governor of Bithynia, when he observed to the Emperor Trajan in AD 109 that the Christians 'met regularly before dawn on a fixed day to chant verses alternately among themselves in honour of Christ as if to a god'.

This call to Spirit-filled worship ends with a focus on a life of thanksgiving. Paul has himself already modelled the importance of continual thanksgiving in 1:16, and emphasised thanksgiving as the hallmark of a life of purity (5:4). The emphasis here in 5:20 on 'always' is a clear indication to embrace a *lifestyle* of thanksgiving. The phrase 'for everything' doesn't, as has sometimes been erroneously taught, mean that we are to give thanks for every circumstance, no matter how bad or tragic, as if God were the direct cause. Rather, we are to give thanks to a good 'God the Father' and to do so in the name of 'our Lord Jesus Christ'; that is, on the basis of who Jesus is and what He has done us.

REFLECT AND RESPOND

- Given this emphasis on worship and thanksgiving, take some time to think about how you can cultivate this more strongly into your life and lifestyle. Consider the following three actions.

- First, make a fresh commitment to regularly participating in corporate worship; come ready and on time to give of yourself to God in worship.

- Second, think how you can include worship and thanksgiving in your devotions – either through reading out passages of praise and thanks from the Bible (such as the Psalms or the 'hymns' of Revelation 4–5) or through musical worship.

- Third, make a choice to develop an 'attitude of gratitude' in all things.

MEMORY VERSE

'Be very careful, then, how you live – not as unwise but as wise'
EPHESIANS 5:15

LIVE A LIFE OF SUBMISSION

'Submit to one another out of reverence for Christ.'
EPHESIANS 5:21

The 2015–2016 English Premier League season was characterised by one of the most surprising achievements in sporting history. Leicester City, a team that spent much of the previous season at the bottom of the league, ended up a year later winning the league – all the more remarkable given that their team was worth a fraction of many of the more famous teams that ended up below them in the table. It seems obvious that their success was not due to the presence of lots of individual superstars, but to the fact that each player consistently played for the whole team and for the manager. The manager, in turn, was credited with adopting an encouraging and fatherly attitude towards his players, genuinely taking an interest in their personal well-being. The success of Leicester City is a heart-warming example of teamwork and mutual respect, in an age which tends to over-celebrate stardom and individual brilliance.

This example of mutual submission is of course neither an isolated one nor a new phenomenon. Nearly 2,000 years ago, writing to ensure the ongoing health and 'success' of the church in Ephesus, Paul urges Christians to 'Submit to one another' but with the greatest motivation of all: 'out of reverence for Christ'. The word 'submit' carries with it the overall meaning of 'placing oneself under', as, for example, soldiers are to 'submit' to their officers in an army.

In addressing the need to submit, Paul is both looking back and looking forwards. First, he is clearly referring back to what he has just been teaching concerning the need for unity in the Church. The word 'submit', literally 'submitting', is the fifth of five participles, which along with speaking, singing, making music and giving thanks, modify the main imperative to be 'filled with the Spirit'. The link is important, because it is only as we are continually filled with the Spirit that we can deny self and submit to one another. The call to submit is in many ways linked right back to 4:1–2 with its emphasis on the character qualities needed to live lives worthy of our calling and to keep the unity of the Spirit in the bond of peace. Like two bookends we have the call to live in humility (4:2) and the call to live in submission (5:21). Both are essential if we are to live in unity, which is of primary concern to Paul and to Jesus. It's only as we do so that we will live in the fullness of God's blessing and 'success' in the Church, which is that it will grow into full maturity in Christ.

Secondly, in calling for Christians to 'Submit to one another' he is also looking forward to the next section (5:22–6:9), where his focus switches from fellowship within the Church to relationships within the home and the workplace. These 'household codes', as they are sometimes called, concern specific instructions given to wives and husbands, to children and parents and to slaves and masters, and are the main focus of next week's study.

For now it's worth emphasising that we are called to a life of submission not just as a hallmark of being filled with the Spirit, but 'out of reverence for Christ'. In the words of Martyn Lloyd-Jones: 'It is only as we are governed by this motive that we shall be able to do all this. A man who is filled with the Spirit is a man who is always remembering the Lord Jesus Christ. The Spirit points to Him, the Spirit glorified Him, the Spirit always leads to Him; and so the man filled with the Spirit will be ever looking at Him. This is his one grand motive – "in the fear of Christ"'.[1] The link between Christ and submission is due to the fact that Christ is the one who has all authority, but humbled Himself as a servant (see Phil. 2:5–11). We are called to live like and honour Him in all our relationships, within the Church, the home and the workplace.

This is deeply challenging to our innate selfishness. As we saw in *Transformed Life* (Day 7), for centuries the Western world thought that the earth, not the sun, was at the centre of the solar system. That was until Copernicus (1473–1543) highlighted that in fact the exact opposite was the case. The letter to the Ephesians, including here in 5:21, is a call to a shift of thinking – from a self-centred to a Christ-centred world-view – and a challenge to live our whole lives, including our relationships, out of 'reverence' for Him.

REFLECT AND RESPOND

- **The heart of submission comes from a heart of humility. How humble are you?**

- **Ask the Lord to forgive you where you have been living selfishly. Rejoice in the fact that He is at the centre, not you!**

MEMORY VERSE

'Be very careful, then, how you live – not as unwise but as wise'
EPHESIANS 5:15

WEEK 6
LIFE IN THE HOME AND THE WORKPLACE

'Wives, submit yourselves to your own husbands as you do to the Lord. For the husband is the head of the wife as Christ is the head of the church, his body, of which he is the Saviour. Now as the church submits to Christ, so also wives should submit to their husbands in everything. Husbands, love your wives, just as Christ loved the church and gave himself up for her to make her holy, cleansing her by the washing with water through the word, and to present her to himself as a radiant church, without stain or wrinkle or any other blemish, but holy and blameless. In this same way, husbands ought to love their wives as their own bodies. He who loves his wife loves himself. After all, no one ever hated their own body, but they feed and care for their body, just as Christ does the church – for we are members of his body. "For this reason a man will leave his father and mother and be united to his wife, and the two will become one flesh." This is a profound mystery – but I am talking about Christ and the church. However, each one of you also must love his wife as he loves himself, and the wife must respect her husband.

Children, obey your parents in the Lord, for this is right. "Honour your father and mother" – which is the first commandment with a promise – "so that it may go well with you and that you may enjoy long life on the earth." Fathers, do not exasperate your children; instead, bring them up in the training and instruction of the Lord.

Slaves, obey your earthly masters with respect and fear, and with sincerity of heart, just as you would obey Christ. Obey them not only to win their favour when their eye is on you, but as slaves of Christ, doing the will of God from your heart. Serve wholeheartedly, as if you were serving the Lord, not people, because you know that the Lord will reward each one for whatever good they do, whether they are slave or free.

And masters, treat your slaves in the same way. Do not threaten them, since you know that he who is both their Master and yours is in heaven, and there is no favouritism with him.'

EPHESIANS 5:22–6:9

CHRISTIAN WIVES

'Wives, submit yourselves to your own husbands as you do to the Lord. For the husband is the head of the wife as Christ is the head of the church, his body, of which he is the Saviour. Now as the church submits to Christ, so also wives should submit to their husbands in everything.' **EPHESIANS 5:22–24**

Children frequently have fascinating perspectives on the subject of human relationships. Here's a couple of thoughts on falling in love: 'It's like an avalanche where you have to run for your life' (John, aged eight); 'No one is sure why it happens, but I heard it has something to do with how you smell ... That's why perfume and deodorant are so popular' (Mae, aged nine). Amusing as this seems, it highlights that we live in a society where there is a great focus on the emotional aspect of 'falling in love'. The problem is that it's just as easy to 'fall out of love'. A staggering 42% of UK marriages end in divorce, and the likelihood of cohabiting couples splitting up is significantly higher. The pain to all concerned – especially as often children are involved in both scenarios – is incalculable.

We could say that there is a battle on for committed life-long marriage relationships. This is nothing new. The apostle Paul, writing in a very different context to believers living in and around first-century Ephesus, placed his significant teaching on marriage and husband–wife relationships (5:22–33), along with instructions to children and parents and slaves and masters (6:1–9), just after his call to wise, Spirit-filled living and just before his teaching on spiritual warfare. In the words of one commentator: 'It is crucial for the various members of the Christian household to be filled with the Spirit (5:18) and to appropriate the enabling power of God (6:10–18) *to resist the attacks of the evil one directed at these important and foundational relationships*'[1] (my italics).

Foremost of these relationships is that between wives and husbands. Before we explore this, let me say a word to those who are single. This passage has a dual application. While addressing the human marriage relationship, Paul makes clear throughout that he is doing so against the backdrop of his primary theme: 'Christ and the church' (5:32). So whether you are married or single, this passage has much to teach us.

Significantly, Paul starts by addressing Christian wives. Against a first-century cultural backdrop where men were frequently viewed as superior to women, and where women were often treated terribly, Paul, like the other biblical writers, took a radically counter-cultural approach which dignified women. The fact that Paul is addressing wives alongside husbands, here in 5:22–24, highlights that women have equal standing before God and in Christ – in itself very counter to the culture of his day. Hence, all that Paul has said thus far about the privileges of being 'in Christ' (chapters 1–3) and the responsibilities of living that out (4:1–5:21) apply equally to men and women. This understanding of our equality in Christ is supported by the clear statement in Paul's letter to the Galatians: 'There is neither Jew nor Gentile, neither slave nor free, nor is there male and female, for you are all one in Christ Jesus' (3:28). In the context of the first century this was quite remarkable, yet is utterly consistent with the broader biblical world-view of men and women as God's image bearers and co-rulers (see Gen. 1–2).

Yet, while dramatically affirming the equality of women with men, Paul also here underscores the fact that they have complementary roles *within marriage*. Again, it is important to note that in a culture where men effectively ruled the household, and women were expected to be subservient, it is significant that Paul urges wives to voluntarily 'submit' to their husbands. However, he does so not as a way of reinforcing cultural norms, but by grounding this in something deeper than culture, the relationship between the Church and Christ – something we will return to in Day 38. The call for wives to submit to their husbands as 'to the Lord' (5:22), has a similar meaning to the previous verse, where all believers were exhorted to submit to one another 'out of reverence for Christ' (5:21). It doesn't mean that wives are to be door-mats, or do things that would be sinful and contrary to what he has already taught in 4:1–5:21. Nor is it a verse saying that all women should submit to all men. Rather, he is treating *Christian* wives with great respect and appealing to them to submit to their husbands, not just because it was the 'right thing to do' culturally, but as a way of expressing their reverence for Christ. This would mean positively respecting their husbands and helping them in their leadership role, praying for them to become all that God wants them to be.

If this can seem challenging, then it was not nearly as challenging as the exhortation to Christian husbands to love their wives as Christ loved the Church. So come back tomorrow to get a fuller picture!

REFLECT AND RESPOND

- If you are married, take time to seek God's wisdom together for the implications of this verse for your marriage. Know that how this will be worked out in practice will depend on the different seasons of life and personalities of different couples.

- If you are a wife, make sure you are regularly praying for your husband, in particular for his faith and spiritual walk, his work, his health, his emotions and, if you have children, his role as father within the family.

- Regardless of whether you are married or not, consider this verse within Paul's broader argument that we are all called to submit to Christ as the head of the Church. Resubmit your life to Christ's lordship today.

MEMORY VERSE

'Submit to one another out of reverence for Christ.'

EPHESIANS 5:21

CHRISTIAN HUSBANDS

'Husbands, love your wives, just as Christ loved the church and gave himself up for her to make her holy, cleansing her by the washing with water through the word, and to present her to himself as a radiant church, without stain or wrinkle or any other blemish, but holy and blameless. In this same way, husbands ought to love their wives as their own bodies. He who loves his wife loves himself. After all, no one ever hated their own body, but they feed and care for their body, just as Christ does the church'
EPHESIANS 5:25–29

I can say that being a husband is one of the most rewarding and challenging aspects of my life. Rewarding, because marriage is a great gift from God, and because Karen is a godly, wise and faithful wife. Challenging, because we are *so* different! For example, Karen is a very practical person and I am a lot less so. It took me a while, therefore, to understand why she considered me bringing her cups of tea in bed such a blessing, and why me not putting the bins out was a cause of some distress! Now married for 30 years, I am still very much on a journey, but I consider loving Karen and meeting her needs to be one of my primary life responsibilities, not just because it is good for our marriage, but because it is a key way that I follow the example of Christ and honour Him.

In our text for today we see how having highlighted the specific responsibility of wives being called to 'submit' to their husbands, Paul gives a far more culturally radical and challenging exhortation: husbands are to 'love' their wives – never the lead title or editorial in *Men's Health* magazine! Jack Hayford helpfully summarises it thus: 'Paul revolutionises the relationship of husbands towards wives in this section. Love, in all of its unconditional facets (Greek *agape*), is the demand put upon the husband. If you were a Greek living in Ephesus, your first response would probably be, "I have to do *what*?"... The expectation of submission from one's wife was easy. That a husband would voluntarily submit to his wife through sacrificial love, thinking only of her benefit, was ridiculous in the ancient male-dominated culture. That a husband must give himself as Christ gave Himself for the church was beyond the imagination of an Ephesian husband.'[1]

This is so important, it needs unpacking. First, the call on husbands to 'love' is not primarily referring to the romantic, sexual way that is so celebrated in our culture today, or the *phileo* (friendship) love that the Stoics encouraged, but is the radical, sacrificial *agape* love that comes from God Himself, and was modelled by Christ. Notice here how 'Christ loved the church', in eternity. Then He 'gave himself for her' by taking on flesh and dying on the cross. Then he cleanses her through the new birth and sanctifies her through the water of the Word. He does all this to present her to himself 'as a radiant church, without stain or wrinkle or any other blemish'. John Stott summarises Christ's love for the Church, and His example of this for Christian husbands: 'The church's head is the church's bridegroom. He does not crush the church. Rather, he sacrificed himself to serve her, in order that she might become everything he longs for her to be, namely herself in the fullness of her glory. Just so a husband should never use his headship to crush or stifle his wife, or frustrate her from being herself. His love for her will lead him to an exactly opposite path. He will give himself for her, in order that she may develop her full potential under God and so become more completely herself.'[2]

If this high ideal of Christ's self-sacrificial love for the Church were not enough, or maybe too lofty to grasp on its own, Paul gives Christian husbands a second and more lowly reason for loving their wives: self-love. We all know how we love ourselves. Hence Paul highlights: 'In this same way, husbands ought to love their wives as their own bodies. He who loves his wife loves himself. After all, no one ever hated their own body, but they feed and care for their body, just as Christ does the church' (5:28–29). Jack Hayford summarises the simple implications of what Paul is saying: 'The truth is that a man cares for himself. Since his wife is part of him, he will care for her in the same way.'[3]

This call to sacrificially love is truly challenging for all Christian husbands. It is not something we can naturally do. It is only possible as we are continually filled with the Spirit (5:18). As we seek God's help, we will be truly honouring and representing Christ well, as well as enabling our wives to become all that God has fully intended for them to be.

REFLECT AND RESPOND

- **If you are a husband, consider how this applies to you today. Are there areas where you have 'crushed', stifled or frustrated your wife, stopping her from becoming who God has called her to be? If so, ask for God's forgiveness (and maybe your wife's!) for where you have failed. Ask for His help and His Spirit.**

- **Whether you are a husband or not, take time to praise God for Christ's love for you as part of His Church – that He loved you, gave Himself up for you, to sanctify and cleanse you, in readiness for presenting you to Himself as perfect on the great, final wedding day. Ask Him to prepare you for the great marriage to come!**

MEMORY VERSE

'Submit to one another out of reverence for Christ.'

EPHESIANS 5:21

CHRISTIAN MARRIAGE

'for we are members of his body. "For this reason a man will leave his father and mother and be united to his wife, and the two will become one flesh." This is a profound mystery – but I am talking about Christ and the church. However, each one of you also must love his wife as he loves himself, and the wife must respect her husband.' **EPHESIANS 5:30–33**

Ruth Graham, the late wife of world-renowned evangelist, Billy Graham, had many relationships and many responsibilities. She married young, supported her husband as he became an international figure, raised their kids, and volunteered in Rev Graham's crusades. Among many attributes, she was known for her tremendous work ethic and her stinging sense of humour. Following Ruth's death in June 2007, friends and family members reminisced about her life. Former first lady, and close personal friend, Barbara Bush recounted a time when Mrs Graham was asked by a writer whether – as a Christian – she had ever contemplated divorce. Barbara quoted the pastor's wife: 'Divorce? No. Murder? Yes.'

Behind this honest and amusing comment lies a clear commitment to the life-long marriage covenant. The apostle Paul here in Ephesians 5 gives us reasons why this is so important.

The first concerns the very sanctity of marriage. The fact that throughout this passage Paul constantly compares the husband–wife relationship to the ultimate picture of Christ and the Church is a stunning affirmation of the wonder of marriage. Here Paul starts by focusing on the relationship between the Church and Christ, by emphasising: 'for we are members of his body'. This clearly picks up on language that he has already used earlier in the letter, with Christ as the supreme head over all and the Church as His body (1:20–23). With this as his primary focus, he then quotes Genesis 2:24 concerning the union of a man and woman in marriage, before concluding: 'this is a profound mystery – but I am talking about Christ and the church'. Given this unashamed and constant linking between marriage and Christ and the Church, we must take very seriously God's intentions for marriage. It is by God's design and we mustn't tamper with it.

The second lesson concerns the idea of the union within marriage. Although Paul here quotes Genesis 2:24 and primarily applies it to Christ and the Church, he well knew that in its original context this is a foundational verse concerning God's intention for human marriage. It is often quoted within the context of a marriage service, with its call for a man to 'leave' his father and mother, and 'cleave', literally be 'glued', to his wife.

This is profound. It certainly involved the 'mysterious and sacred depths of sexual union',[1] a joining that is more than just physical, but a deep coming together of two persons at an emotional and even spiritual level. Sex is a holy act, and is reserved for marriage between a husband and wife. For it to be used in any other way will lead to a lot of harm as two parts try to become 'unglued'.

The third lesson concerns equality and complementarity within marriage. As we saw on Day 29, the equality of wives and husbands is evident in that they are part of the same body of Christ, are called to 'be filled' with the same Spirit (5:18), and are part of the same community who are urged to 'submit to one another out of reverence for Christ' (5:21). The fact that Paul is addressing wives as well as husbands highlights that before God they are of equal standing. Yet in their equality there is also difference and complementarity. Hence, once again, Paul re-iterates the differing exhortations to husbands and wives. Here in verse 33, he starts with the husbands, who have been the main focus of his attention from verse 25, reminding them of their radical call to unconditionally 'love' their wives. Then he proceeds to the wives, with a slight nuance that they are to 'respect' their husbands. This word used is different to the call to 'submit', but relates back to 5:21, where all members of the body are to submit 'out of reverence [respect] for Christ'. So both husbands and wives are not to love and respect or submit for the sake of cultural conformity, or just as a duty, but out of loving respect for Christ, who has so blessed them, loved them, and saved them by His amazing grace.

But remember: all of this is ultimately a picture of Christ and the Church!

REFLECT AND RESPOND

- **If you are married, take time to prayerfully examine your relationship. Talk together, pray together, get help if needed. Read good books on relationships such as Gary Chapman's *The Five Love Languages: How to Express Heartfelt Commitment to Your Mate* or Tim Keller's *The Meaning of Marriage*. Why not go on a Marriage Course? Do whatever it takes to enhance your marriage. It's not just good for you (and others!), but is a great way of you expressing your love and honour of Christ.**

- **If you are not married, reflect once again on the amazing privilege that you have in being a member of Christ's body, and of the ultimate prize of oneness with Him, both now and for eternity. Do all that you can to submit to and honour Him as your head!**

MEMORY VERSE

'Submit to one another out of reverence for Christ.'

EPHESIANS 5:21

CHRISTIAN CHILDREN

'Children, obey your parents in the Lord, for this is right. "Honour your father and mother" – which is the first commandment with a promise – "so that it may go well with you and that you may enjoy long life on the earth."' **EPHESIANS 6:1–3**

Having talked about the responsibilities of wives and husbands, Paul now moves on to a discussion about children and parents. As with the section on wives and husbands he starts with what in that culture would have been perceived as the socially 'lesser' group: children. It is worth noting at the outset that the fact that he is addressing children at all, and addressing them first, is a way of acknowledging and honouring them. It indicates that children were a recognised group within the 'one body' of Christ, and that presumably they would have been part of gatherings where this letter would have been read out.

The same overall context applies to children as to wives, in that they are to live out their responsibility as part of their overall role of being very careful to live in wisdom (5:15), to be filled with the Spirit (5:18), and to express this in submission to others out of reverence for Christ. However, the exhortation is much stronger. Whereas wives are to submit to and respect their husbands (as part of a one flesh union), children are to 'obey' and 'honour'.

First, the call to 'obey' applies to children who are under their parents' direct responsibility. How this applies varies from culture to culture. In modern Western contexts, for example, we would say this is until they come of age, or practically leave home and maybe get married. More broadly, the obedience of children to parents was something that was assumed in the different cultures of the ancient world and indeed in most cultures throughout history. So, when Paul says, 'obey your parents … for this is right' he is on one level affirming what is right in 'natural law', that which is obvious. But, as with the other exhortations, he is applying this in a specifically Christian context, since this obedience is to be done 'in the Lord'. In other words, Christian children are treated here with dignity. They are not just told to obey because they must do what they are told(!) but they are to obey because they are Christians, who are honouring Christ by obeying their parents. This phrase 'in the Lord', similar to with wives, qualifies the fact that obedience would not mean obeying sinful commands, or commands that directly compromise their higher obedience to Christ.

The second call to 'honour' applies to all children: both to younger children – since their obedience needs to be genuine and from the heart – and to older ones even when they have come of age. Here Paul quotes a compilation of Greek texts, Exodus 20:12 with Deuteronomy 5:16, to emphasise the importance of honouring one's parents, which contains a dual promise. The fact that Paul quotes from what is one of the Ten Commandments highlights the importance and seriousness of this command. Christians have sometimes divided the commandments into two uneven sections, the first four relating to our duty to love God, and the remaining six to our call to love our neighbour. This fifth commandment is seen to relate to our duty to our neighbour. However, the Jews regularly taught that the Law had two tablets, each containing five commandments. This means that the honouring of our parents is part of the first tablet and directly related to our responsibility towards God Himself. This serves to highlight that, especially during childhood, parents are there to represent God to their children and to mediate His love and authority towards them. Hence, disobedience to and dishonouring of parents was treated very seriously in the Old Testament, since this was seen as disobeying and dishonouring God.

Significantly, though, Paul encourages Christian children 'in the Lord', not through warnings, but with a promise. The first aspect of this is a promise of blessing: 'that it may go well with you'. Rather than over-spiritualise this promise as concerning 'eternal' life, it should be understood as conveying blessing in the broadest context possible in this life. Similarly, the second promise of longevity, 'that you may enjoy long life on the earth', is to be understood as meaning just that: fruitful and full life in this life! Jack Hayford summarises the importance of this: 'This is a law that is woven into the fabric of the universe. People cannot dishonour their parents and realise fruitfulness or fullness in life.'[1] Although, as C.E. Arnold rightly comments: 'This cannot, of course, be applied in a meticulous way to every single case. Like any proverb, this is to be understood as a general pattern. Exceptions to the rule will take place.'[2]

REFLECT AND RESPOND

- **If you are a still under your parents' care, reflect carefully on this passage. What can you do to 'obey' and 'honour' your parents?**

- **We all need to honour our parents, regardless of our age. If your parents are still alive, show them respect and kindness, and support them as they grow older.**

MEMORY VERSE

'Submit to one another out of reverence for Christ.'
EPHESIANS 5:21

CHRISTIAN PARENTS

'Fathers, do not exasperate your children; instead, bring them up in the training and instruction of the Lord.' **EPHESIANS 6:4**

Apart from being a disciple of Jesus, and a husband of Karen, my life's greatest privilege and responsibility has been as a dad of two daughters. Like all parents I can look back and think of things I would do differently, but I am particularly glad that while the girls were still very young, I made the decision to be an active rather than an absentee dad. While Karen invested most of her time, especially in their pre-school years, I also played my part in their emotional and spiritual development. One very important decision I made was that, while Karen was out at worship practice, I dedicated Thursday nights as 'daddy–daughter' nights. On a weekly basis, I would spend time with the girls, eating food and often watching films together. These started with *Thomas the Tank Engine*, *Bambi*, *Dumbo* and *Pinocchio*, before progressing to certain 'chick flicks'. Top of the list was *The Parent Trap*, which I must have watched a dozen times! Now with the girls both happily married, I look back and am so grateful for those years of investment, which also included times of worship, reading the Bible to them and prayer.

Here in Ephesians 6:4, having talked to Christian children about their responsibility to obey and honour their parents (6:1–3), Paul now moves on to address the role of Christian parents. Although it is possible to understand the word 'fathers' in a generic sense as referring to 'parents', as some translations have it, it seems most likely that Paul is focusing on fathers. The question then needs to be addressed: why? And why not mothers? It is likely to be because in Roman and in Jewish society fathers were seen as ultimately responsible for the education and discipline of their children.[1]

We need to realise, once again, how radical and counter-cultural Paul's word to fathers was. The picture of fathers as self-controlled, 'gentle, patient educators of their children' is in stark contrast to the norm of his day,[2] where the father exercised sovereign authority over all members of his family: 'Completely different was the Christian father', given that his fatherhood was rooted in the fatherhood of God (see 3:14–15; 4:6).[3]

So let's look at the exhortations given for the Christian father. First, fathers are instructed not to 'exasperate' their children. For a first-century father this would have probably come as a surprise, since it was generally assumed that children were more likely to frustrate their fathers through disobedience and rebellion. In the parallel passage in Colossians 3:21, Paul writes: 'Fathers, do not embitter you children, or they will become discouraged.' This curbing of parental authority highlights that although children are to obey their parents in the Lord, they too have a life and personality of their own: 'They are little people in their own right. As such they are to be respected, and on no account to be exploited, manipulated or crushed.'[4]

Fathers are also exhorted to positively invest in their children and to 'bring them up in the training and instruction of the Lord'. This includes the idea of nourishing or feeding. John Calvin translates this as: 'Let them be only cherished … deal gently with them.'[5] Within this context of love and care, there is the need for training or discipline. This concerns the need to establish and enforce clear boundaries. Then there is the call to give instruction. This is important. Although teachers at school and Sunday school can have a huge influence on our children, it is vital that parents don't abdicate their primary responsibility. The addition of the phrase 'of the Lord' implies not just that we should bring them up in a godly way, but that they will personally know the Lord and embrace His ways.

REFLECT AND RESPOND

- If you are a parent with children still at home, ask God for His strength and grace to be able to represent Him well and mediate love to your children in the way that He does.

- If you have grown-up children, pray regularly for them, that they would walk in God's perfect plans.

- If you do not have children, thank God that He is your Father. Ask for His help to become a spiritual father or mother to many!

MEMORY VERSE

'Submit to one another out of reverence for Christ.'

EPHESIANS 5:21

CHRISTIAN SLAVES

'Slaves, obey your earthly masters with respect and fear, and with sincerity of heart, just as you would obey Christ. Obey them not only to win their favour when their eye is on you, but as slaves of Christ, doing the will of God from your heart. Serve wholeheartedly, as if you were serving the Lord, not people, because you know that the Lord will reward each one for whatever good they do, whether they are slave or free.' **EPHESIANS 6:5–8**

For the first four years while we were establishing the church in Peterborough, I worked as a history teacher. Being a Christian in the workplace was both challenging and very rewarding. One of the greatest challenges was just the relentless pressure of working in a school that had Monday through till Saturday morning lessons and lots of marking! There were times when I felt utterly exhausted. But there was also an overall sense of fulfilment, knowing that for this season of my life I was called to do this and that I was working for Christ as my ultimate boss. This helped me in giving my best without allowing work to dominate my life and hinder my time with God, my family and the local church. It also helped me to honour those in authority, ensuring that I refused to get involved in gossip and negative criticism of the headmaster and those in charge. As a 'witness' for Christ in the workplace, while careful not to abuse my position by inappropriately 'preaching' to those I was teaching, I did prayerfully seek opportunities to testify of Him. I recently heard a wonderful story of one of my pupils who came to Christ. Unbeknown to me, his first 'stirring' of faith came as I used the 'Bridge Diagram' to explain what the sixteenth-century reformers meant by salvation through faith in Christ alone!

This whole issue of how we live our Christian lives at work is certainly one of huge importance. Having spent time on relationships within the home, Paul moves on to focus on relationships within the workplace. In particular, he focuses in on the responsibilities of Christian slaves and their masters. The fact that Paul addresses slaves and masters (6:5–9) can seem strange and even shocking to modern ears, especially as many Christian organisations, churches and individuals are rightly at the forefront of the fight against modern-day slavery.

However, before we jump to any wrong conclusions it is important to note the very different cultural context that Paul was writing in. Put simply, slavery in the ancient world was a significant and accepted part of the socio-economic system of the day, with some estimating that one-third of the population of the city of Rome was made up of slaves, and that there may have been 60 million slaves in the Roman Empire as a whole. Paul here in Ephesians is not endorsing the system per se; rather he is recognising that this situation exists, and seeking to give instructions about right attitudes to *Christian* slaves and masters. The fact that he addresses slaves at all (as he has done with wives and children), is in itself remarkable, giving them huge dignity and equal standing within the Christian community. Moreover, it is very significant he does *not* give a theological basis for slavery as he does for marriage (5:22–33). Rather, he simply gives instructions for how to live within this system. Elsewhere, notably in 1 Corinthians 7:21, he states: 'Were you a slave when you were called? Don't let it trouble you – although if you can gain your freedom, do so.' More striking still is Paul's beautiful little letter to Philemon, in which he urges Philemon to receive back his fugitive but now converted slave Onesimus, and to welcome him 'no longer as a slave, but better than a slave, as a dear brother'. By way of emphasis, Paul adds: 'He is very dear to me but even dearer to you, both as a fellow man and as a brother in the Lord' (Philem. 1:16). John Stott rightly comments: 'The words would have sounded incredible to all but Christian ears … A message which thus united master and slaves as brothers … issued a radical challenge to an institution which separated them as proprietor and property.'[1]

This broader New Testament context is important in understanding the passage here in Ephesians. The emphasis is not just that slaves should obey their masters: culturally they were expected to do that. Rather, remarkably, Christian slaves are addressed as full members of the Church community and urged to obey with a genuineness and sincerity that comes out of their relationship with Christ: a fact highlighted in references to Christ or 'the Lord' in all four of these verses (6:5–8). The message is clear: as slaves obeyed their masters from their hearts they were honouring Christ, their ultimate master, and they would receive His reward.

Although the circumstances are very different, we can apply a number of the principles to employee–employer relationships. One commentator, C.E. Arnold, has helpfully summarised this:

1. *'Treat your managers or supervisors with respect'*, not due to whether you think they deserve it, but because of their position of responsibility over you.
2. *'Do your work with a pure heart and good attitude.'*
3. *'Don't perform just to make a good impression.'* This applies when our bosses are not present, since we are ultimately working for the Lord and He sees everything and deserves our best!
4. *'Give God's will top priority in your life and work.'*
5. *'Remember that the Lord expects us to do good works, notices when we do them, and will reward all that we have done.'*[2]

REFLECT AND RESPOND

- Which of those five points would you like to grow in?

- If you are working for a supervisor or manager, take time today to seek the Lord. Ask God to speak to you about your working life and attitude to your boss. Ask for forgiveness if you have been lacking and ask for His help, knowing that it is ultimately Christ you are serving.

- If you are faithfully working in a tough situation, be encouraged that you will receive a great reward from the Lord!

MEMORY VERSE

'Submit to one another out of reverence for Christ.'

EPHESIANS 5:21

CHRISTIAN MASTERS

'And masters, treat your slaves in the same way.
Do not threaten them, since you know that he who is
both their Master and yours is in heaven, and there
is no favouritism with him.' **EPHESIANS 6:9**

The Cadbury family, with their Quaker beliefs that all human beings
should be treated equally and should live in peace, exemplified this in
the way they treated their employees. Their first shop was opened in
1824 and by the 1870s their chocolate and cocoa business had grown
to the point where they needed to expand, and so they purchased
some land in the countryside outside Birmingham, in an area that
became known as Bournville. There they built not just a new factory
but a village where their workers could live, and the estate included an
area for parks, recreation grounds and open space. The Cadburys set
new standards for working and living conditions in Victorian Britain
and the Cadbury plant in Bournville became known as 'the factory in
a garden'. Subsequent generations of the Cadbury family also took on
the responsibility for their workers, from ensuring pensions were set
up, to founding colleges in the local community.

The apostle Paul would have heartily approved of the way that the
Cadburys treated their workers. Writing in the very different cultural
context of ancient Rome, Paul concludes his household section by
addressing a sixth group: 'And masters, treat your slaves in the same
way. Do not threaten them, since you know that he who is both their
Master and yours is in heaven, and there is no favouritism with him.'

Although, in context, this applies specifically to the master–slave system of the day, there are a number of transferable principles into our world today with reference to the conduct of managers and supervisors.

The first concerns the command for masters to treat their slaves 'in the same way'. This is a hugely important and, once again, radically counter-cultural exhortation: 'It is an application of the golden rule. However masters hope their slaves will behave towards them, they must behave towards their slaves in the same way. Paul admits no privileged superiority in the masters, as if they could themselves dispense with the very courtesies they expect to be shown'.[1]

The second principle concerns the command: 'Do not threaten them'. The masters are not to misuse their position of authority by issuing threats of punishment. Punishment was accepted in the empire as the only way to keep slaves in order. Without forbidding punishment per se, Paul is warning the powerful against wrongly threatening the powerless. In a modern-day work context, we could say that generally people thrive in an atmosphere of love and positive encouragement. That doesn't mean that it is wrong to hold people accountable, and, if all else fails, issue genuine warnings for poor performance, but using hasty or casual 'threats' is wrong.

The third principle concerns the motivation for the first two: 'since you know that he who is both their Master and yours is in heaven, and there is no favouritism with him'. Again, in the culture of the day, this was a radically levelling statement. To Christian masters (and employers), there is the strong reminder that their Christian slaves (and employees) have the same master who is in heaven. Slave owners were used to being flattered, but they are clearly told that they will not receive such discriminatory favouritism from the Lord.

John Stott helpfully concludes: 'Thus all three principles were designed to lessen the cultural and social gap between slave and slave-owner. Instead of regarding his relationship with his slaves as that of proprietor to chattels, or of superior to inferiors, he was to develop a relationship in which he gave them *the same* treatment as he hoped to receive, renounced the unfair weapon of threats, and recalled that he and they both shared the same heavenly master and impartial judge'.[2] This conclusion concerning the goal of lessening the 'social gap' could be applied in many ways to the relationship between wives and husbands, children and parents, too. As we've already seen in Galatians 3:28, Paul is clear that in the Christian community: 'There is neither Jew nor Gentile, neither slave nor free, nor is there male and female, for you are all one in Christ Jesus.'

REFLECT AND RESPOND

- **If you are an employer, supervisor or manager, consider carefully what attitudes you display towards those who are working for you. Prayerfully ask the Lord for His help to become more Christlike in your oversight of those under your leadership, supervision and care.**

- **If you are an employee, pray regularly for those leading you: for wisdom, favour and blessing on them and their families, and the ability to lead their teams effectively.**

MEMORY VERSE

'Submit to one another out of reverence for Christ.'
EPHESIANS 5:21

WEEK 7
THE ARMOUR OF GOD

'Finally, be strong in the Lord and in his mighty power. Put on the full armour of God, so that you can take your stand against the devil's schemes. For our struggle is not against flesh and blood, but against the rulers, against the authorities, against the powers of this dark world and against the spiritual forces of evil in the heavenly realms. Therefore put on the full armour of God, so that when the day of evil comes, you may be able to stand your ground, and after you have done everything, to stand. Stand firm then, with the belt of truth buckled round your waist, with the breastplate of righteousness in place, and with your feet fitted with the readiness that comes from the gospel of peace. In addition to all this, take up the shield of faith, with which you can extinguish all the flaming arrows of the evil one. Take the helmet of salvation and the sword of the Spirit, which is the word of God.

And pray in the Spirit on all occasions with all kinds of prayers and requests. With this in mind, be alert and always keep on praying for all the Lord's people. Pray also for me, that whenever I speak, words may be given me so that I will fearlessly make known the mystery of the gospel, for which I am an ambassador in chains. Pray that I may declare it fearlessly, as I should.'

EPHESIANS 6:10–20

DAY 43

BE STRONG, PUT ON THE FULL ARMOUR, TAKE YOUR STAND

'Finally, be strong in the Lord and in his mighty power. Put on the full armour of God, so that you can take your stand against the devil's schemes.'
EPHESIANS 6:10–11

On D-Day, 6 June 1944, the Allies successfully landed on the Normandy beaches, thus opening up a second front against Nazi Germany, thereby ensuring that Hitler would eventually be defeated. However, it took eleven more months of hard fighting before the war in Europe finally ended on VE Day, 8 May 1945. This is a great picture of the battle that we are involved in as Christians, and fits in well with Paul's description of this in Ephesians. In 1:19–23 and 2:4–6 we see how much has *already* been accomplished in the spiritual D-Day when God victoriously raised Christ from the dead and seated Him far above all principalities and powers (see *Transformed Life* Day 21). This means that all of those who are now 'in Christ' *already* share in His victory since they have been made spiritually alive and are now seated with Him in heavenly places (see 2:4–6). However, Paul is also very much aware that while the ultimate battle has been won, there is *still* an intense, ongoing spiritual warfare prior to the final Victory Day, when Christ will return.

This emphasis on spiritual warfare is given not to alarm us but to alert us to the reality of what we are engaged in. The first-century Christians in and around Ephesus would have been fully aware of this, given that many of them had been saved out of an occult background where other gods and goddesses were freely worshipped and celebrated (see Acts 19). Yet the challenge to continue the battle and live in spiritual victory is something that is timeless for all eras and cultures, including our own. So how are we to live out Christ's victory against spiritual opposition? Paul highlights three things.

First, we are to 'be strong in the Lord and in his mighty power'. The 'Lord' here is the Lord Jesus Christ and highlights that we are not in a hopeless fight against a fearsome enemy but rather we can be strong 'in the Lord' and in His authority since we are seated with Him in heavenly places. We also are to be strong 'in his mighty power'. This focus on the Lord's power runs right through Ephesians 1–3, with Paul keen to highlight how those who have been spiritually raised with Christ have the same power that raised Christ from the dead (1:19–20). This power is not just something that we *have* received through our new birth (2:4–6), but that we are to *keep on receiving* through the person and presence of the Holy Spirit. So much so that Paul prays – and we must pray – that the Father would strengthen us 'with power through his Spirit' (3:16), and ensure that we are continually filled with the Spirit on a daily basis (5:18). Yes, we are in a fight, but we have Christ's authority and power to enable us to win!

Second, we must 'put on the full armour of God'. It seems very likely that Paul was making reference to the armour and weapons worn by the Roman soldiers of his day. His hearers – Jew and Gentile – would immediately have identified with the picture of a fully equipped Roman legionary standing alongside his fellow soldiers in a near invincible cohort. Yet, as well as this contemporary picture, Paul is basing his description on something more ancient and far more powerful, which is the 'armour of God' as described by Isaiah (Isa. 11:5; 52:7; 59:17). Hence, the image is that just as God is depicted as a warrior who puts on righteousness, faithfulness, peace and salvation, so we must put on the same armour, which He now provides for us. We will return to the theme of the armour of God throughout this week, but for now it's important to stress that we must wear the armour if we are to prevail.

Third, once we are living in Christ's victory, exercising our new authority and power in Him, and wearing God's full armour, we will be able to take our stand against the devil's schemes. Tomorrow we will look more fully at the enemy that we face, but here Paul reminds us that we have an enemy, the devil, and that he has 'schemes' against the people of God. We must be alert to this, but not be fearful, knowing that we can and will 'stand'.

Finally, we must note that the imperatives throughout this section are plural. Without denying the relevance of these instructions for us as individual Christians, it is important that Paul's overall concern is that the Church collectively be strong, put on God's armour and stand as one.

REFLECT AND RESPOND

- **Thank God for the privilege of being 'in Christ' – of being seated and secure in Him.**

- **Pray for yourself and others in your small group and church; that you and they may be strengthened in the Lord and in His mighty power.**

- **Make a decision today that you are going to stand against the devil's schemes.**

MEMORY VERSE

'Finally, be strong in the Lord and in his mighty power. Put on the full armour of God, so that you can take your stand against the devil's schemes.'

EPHESIANS 6:10–11

THE REALITY OF THE OPPOSITION, THE ASSURANCE OF VICTORY

'For our struggle is not against flesh and blood, but against the rulers, against the authorities, against the powers of this dark world and against the spiritual forces of evil in the heavenly realms. Therefore put on the full armour of God, so that when the day of evil comes, you may be able to stand your ground, and after you have done everything, to stand.' **EPHESIANS 6:12–13**

In the Korean War, a group of US soldiers known as Baker Company found themselves cut off from the rest of their unit, in the face of an enemy advance. For several hours no word was heard, even though headquarters repeatedly tried to communicate with the missing troops. At last a weak signal was received. The corpsman asked, 'Baker Company, do you read me?'

'This is Baker Company,' they replied.

'What is your situation?' the corpsman asked.

'The enemy is to the east of us, the enemy is to the west of us, the enemy is to the north of us, the enemy is to the south of us.'

Then after a brief pause, the sergeant determinedly said, 'The enemy is not going to get away from us now!' I like this faith-filled realism![1]

In a somewhat similar way, Paul here in Ephesians 6:12–13 is concerned to wake us up to the reality of the opposition that we face, not as grounds for fear, but as a motivation to action, leading to victory. It highlights how important it is that we get a right balance when thinking about spiritual evil. As C.S. Lewis has pointed out: 'There are two equal and opposite errors into which our race can fall about the devils. One is to disbelieve in their existence. The other is to believe, and to feel an excessive and unhealthy interest in them. They themselves are equally pleased by both errors, and hail a materialist or magician with the same delight.'[2] When I first became a Christian, I fell into the first error as, for the early months of my walk, I didn't even believe that the devil existed! My objection was primarily theological – a view that quickly changed once I accepted the full authority of Scripture. While most Christians would not theologically disbelieve in the existence of evil, many live their lives *practically* as if the devil and demons don't exist, thus completely underplaying or underestimating their foes. Others are all too aware of the existence of evil, but fall into the opposite error of an over-emphasis on the demonic and either through fear or fascination, give too much credit to the devil and his power – ending up in a form of dualism, with God and the devil erroneously thought of as equal combatants.

Here in these verses, Paul presents a wonderfully balanced view. To those of us who are tempted to deny or underplay the existence of evil, verse 12 alerts us to the existence of the enemy that we face. Notice that our warfare is 'not against flesh and blood' but 'against the rulers, against the authorities, against the powers of this dark world and against the spiritual forces of evil in the heavenly realms'. It's not people who are our enemies, but the devil (see 6:11), and those other spiritual forces of evil that operate under his authority. We are to 'wrestle' against this spiritual opposition, implying that the combat is often close and intense. All of this is not to frighten us but to alert us to the facts, since if we don't have a proper understanding of our spiritual opposition, we will not be sufficiently empowered, equipped and ready to win!

Verse 13 refers to 'the day of evil'. This could mean the general times that we are living in, prior to the second coming of Christ, when the devil still has some sway in the world. But it also highlights that there can be times in the lives of individual believers and churches when the enemy's attack seems particularly fierce. That's the bad news!

But the very good news is that Paul is telling us this because he expects us to win! He doesn't want us to fear, or to be over-preoccupied with the enemy. He certainly doesn't want us to elevate the devil and his minions to an equal place with Christ, or with us as Christians, who are now seated with Christ in the heavenly places (see Day 43). He does, however, want us to be prepared, to understand the urgent necessity of putting on the full armour of God, and having done all of this to stand and stand firm. This call to stand appears here twice, and four times in this section as a whole (vv11,13–14). It means that since Christ has won the victory, we have to stand, maintain and enforce it!

REFLECT AND RESPOND

- **Which of the two extremes – underplaying or overplaying the existence of evil – are you more likely to fall into? Ask the Lord to help you get the right balance.**

- **If you are going through a particularly challenging time in your life, and feel under or are aware of a spiritual attack, determine that you are not going to fear, but that you are going to stand firm. Share your struggle with others in your small group or church family and have them stand with you, too.**

MEMORY VERSE

'Finally, be strong in the Lord and in his mighty power. Put on the full armour of God, so that you can take your stand against the devil's schemes.'

EPHESIANS 6:10–11

THE BELT OF TRUTH, THE BREASTPLATE OF RIGHTEOUSNESS

'Stand firm then, with the belt of truth buckled round your waist, with the breastplate of righteousness in place' **EPHESIANS 6:14**

Having laid a foundation for understanding our call to spiritual warfare (vv10–13), Paul now reminds us of the call to stand (for a fourth time!), and begins to look at the armour in more detail. In the following verses (14–17), he highlights six pieces of armour. Today we will examine the first two: the belt of truth and the breastplate of righteousness. Before we look at each in turn it's important to note the belt needs to be 'buckled' and the breastplate put 'in place'. Truth and righteousness have to be operating in our lives for us to enjoy God's protection and victory.

First, Paul refers to the 'belt of truth'. The belt is used to convey the idea of tying around the waist, which in the ancient world meant tying up long robes in readiness for action. For soldiers, it most likely referred to a leather apron-like covering tied around the waist to protect the lower abdomen. Throughout Ephesians, Paul is very insistent on the importance of us living in the truth. In the words of one commentator: 'Paul was deeply concerned about the variety of ways that the devil schemes and strategises to misrepresent, deceive, and trick believers. Because of this, he wants them to be fully convinced of the truth of the gospel and the truth about their new identity in Jesus Christ.'[1] Over the years, I have personally found that the more I get to know and walk with Jesus, who is the Truth (John 14:6), and the more time I spend in the truth of His Word, the Bible, the more my whole life is secured by the belt of truth.

Of course, it's not just enough to know *about* the truth, we must also live our lives *in accordance with* the truth. We have already seen that lying, deception and the speaking of falsehood have no place in the life of a believer or in the Church of Jesus Christ (4:25). Instead we are called to speak and live the truth.

Second, Paul highlights the 'breastplate of righteousness'. In Roman armour, the breastplate was the piece that covered the whole chest area, protecting many of the vital organs, including the heart. In the same way it is vital that we wear the breastplate of righteousness for our spiritual protection. So what is this 'righteousness'? In the context of Isaiah, where God puts on 'righteousness as his breastplate' (59:17), it refers to God's justice. Paul, however, in his wider writings, refers to God's righteousness or justice not as something we have to attain to, but as a gift that we receive through faith (see Rom. 3:21–22; 5:1,17–21). This is so crucial to grasp since one of the strategies of the devil, the accuser or slanderer, is to question our new identity in Christ, especially our being made righteous in Him. I remember as a very young Christian how my early months of discipleship were characterised by me making some spiritual progress but also frequently getting 'hit' with condemnation and a sense of guilt that I was not living up to God's high standard. Then one day when I was in a group Bible study on the book of Romans, I had a revelation of God's righteousness as a gift to be received through faith in Christ. From then on, everything changed. For most of the last 30 years, I have enjoyed the benefit of having the breastplate of righteousness firmly in place and have lived free, knowing that 'there is now no condemnation for those who are in Christ Jesus' (Rom. 8:1).

This emphasis from the book of Romans very much fits with Paul's 'in Christ' teaching in the earlier chapters of Ephesians. But in the context of Ephesians as a whole, it is important to extend the focus on the gift of righteousness, to us living in practical righteousness or holiness. For example, we are exhorted to put on the new self 'created to be like God in true *righteousness* and holiness' (4:24, my emphasis) and to live as children of the light since 'the fruit of the light consists in all goodness, *righteousness* and truth' (5:9, my emphasis). In summary, to put on the breastplate of righteousness refers to both us having received the gift of righteousness, and living righteously. In the words of one commentator: 'The completeness of pardon for past offence and integrity of character that belong to the justified life, are woven together into an impenetrable mail'.[2]

REFLECT AND RESPOND

- **How can you grow in truth? Consider how you can continue and increase your investment in the Word of God beyond this 50-day study.**

- **Are you clear in your understanding that you have been made 'righteous' in Christ? Reread Romans 8:1, and thank God that in Christ you are no longer under condemnation.**

- **Ask God to fill you again with His Spirit and to help you grow in living *in* the truth and *in* righteousness in all areas of your life.**

- Say this prayer: 'I put on the belt of truth around my waist. Help me, Lord, to listen to and act on Your truth alone and not be deceived by the devil's lies. I put on the breastplate of righteousness. Thank You, Lord, that because of Your redemption, I am righteous in Christ. Help me live my life in a way that honours You. Amen.'

MEMORY VERSE

'Finally, be strong in the Lord and in his mighty power. Put on the full armour of God, so that you can take your stand against the devil's schemes.'

EPHESIANS 6:10–11

THE READINESS OF THE GOSPEL OF PEACE, THE SHIELD OF FAITH

'and with your feet fitted with the readiness that comes from the gospel of peace. In addition to all this, take up the shield of faith, with which you can extinguish all the flaming arrows of the evil one.'
EPHESIANS 6:15–16

We continue to look at the call to stand and prevail against our spiritual enemies by putting on the full armour of God. Here, specifically, we will be focusing on the next two parts of the armour: the readiness of the gospel of peace and the shield of faith.

First, what does it mean to have our 'feet fitted with the readiness that comes from the gospel of peace'? Although the actual footwear isn't mentioned, it is likely that Paul has in mind a Roman soldier's leather boots with studs on the sole and heel to improve his footing. The key idea here is one of readiness. It's possible that this readiness is something that we have as a result of us receiving the message of the gospel of peace. However, it is more likely that it should be best understood as 'the readiness to announce the Good News of peace' (GNB). This is more in line with the prophecy of Isaiah, which clearly stands behind this passage – in particular, Isaiah 52:7: 'How beautiful on the mountains are the feet of those who bring good news, who proclaim peace, who bring good tidings, who proclaim salvation, who say to Zion, "Your God reigns!"' Paul quotes this in Romans 10:15 in connection with the proclamation of the gospel of Jesus Christ. Here in Ephesians 6:15, this emphasis on being ready to proclaim the gospel of peace is set within the specific context of spiritual warfare. In summary, it means the following: at the heart of the gospel is the message that Christ is now our 'peace' and has reconciled us to God, and to one another (Eph. 2:14–18). This is such good news that we must be ever-ready to share it. As we do so, we help liberate those who are held captive by the spiritual forces of evil.

The key point is that we need to be in a state of readiness. A soldier named Brian McCoic, 1st sergeant in Charlie Company, 6th Engineer Support Battalion, talked of his experience of being a marine for 19 years and the need to be combat ready. In an interview he shared how he sleeps fully dressed, wearing his boots, so that 'I can go from zero to awake pretty quickly'.[1] Many times as Christians, when it comes to sharing our testimony and the gospel with others, our main issue is not that we lack motivation or love for the lost, but rather that we are simply not combat ready. In fact, sometimes we are effectively sleeping and so opportunities catch us unaware. Like McCoic, we need to ensure our feet are fitted with the readiness that comes from the gospel of peace, so that we can go from 'zero to awake' when opportunities arise.

Second, what does it mean 'to take up the shield of faith' and thereby 'extinguish all the flaming arrows of the evil one'? The shield was an important piece of defensive weaponry used by all armies in the ancient world. In the Roman army the shield was large and rectangular, under which a soldier could be completely protected from the enemy's arrows. In addition, the outside of the shield would be covered in calf skin and dampened so as to put out the flaming arrows which were sometimes fired.[2]

Here we see faith like a mighty shield sufficient to deal with all the deadly attacks of the evil one. This faith is not just referring to objective faith or truth, but is our personal faith or trust in God and His promises.

It is not our faith in our faith, but our faith in God, who is our great protector. I know that for me personally, there have been many times when simple faith in God and His promises have kept me going and kept us on track as a church, when we have been assaulted by 'flaming arrows' from the evil one. One incident immediately comes to mind. We were in a critical phase of securing land and beginning to lay foundations for our KingsGate Peterborough building and all was not going according to plan. Karen and I were away with the leadership team at a conference, and both found ourselves lying awake being bombarded with fear and intimidation from the enemy. When we recognised what was going on, we prayed together, lifting up our shield of faith in God and His promises. As we did so, we were we immediately conscious of the 'flaming arrows' of the evil one being extinguished.

REFLECT AND RESPOND

- **How would you describe your state of readiness to share the gospel? Pray, asking God to give you opportunities to share the good news, and prepare yourself to be ready!**

- **Are there any areas where you are currently being bombarded with the flaming arrows of the evil one? Take time to reaffirm your faith in God and remember His promises for your life.**

- **Say this prayer: 'I put on the shoes of the gospel of peace. Lord, I am willing to go anywhere You ask or do anything You ask of me. I stand behind the shield of faith, secure in the knowledge of Your goodness, love and power. Amen.'**

MEMORY VERSE

'Finally, be strong in the Lord and in his mighty power. Put on the full armour of God, so that you can take your stand against the devil's schemes.'

EPHESIANS 6:10–11

THE HELMET OF SALVATION, THE SWORD OF THE SPIRIT

'Take the helmet of salvation and the sword of the Spirit, which is the word of God.' **EPHESIANS 6:17**

Here Paul highlights the importance of the fifth and sixth weapons: the helmet of salvation and the sword of the Spirit.

First, note the vital importance of wearing the helmet of salvation. In the world of motorcycling, some statistics suggest that 75% of fatalities and over 85% of all bike-related injuries would be prevented if riders wore helmets. In life and in the arena of spiritual warfare, it is similarly vital that we wear our protective head-gear or helmet. The helmet that the Roman soldiers would have worn offered vital protection for the head and parts of the face. In Isaiah, we see a picture of God wearing 'the helmet of salvation' as He saves His people and judges their enemies (59:17). Here in Ephesians God has given us this helmet of salvation as a way of protecting us, most likely in the key battleground of our minds. The point seems clear: if our minds can stay protected, we will go a long way to winning in all areas of our lives.

So what is the 'salvation' that Paul is referring to? Elsewhere in his writings, the helmet of salvation is a sure knowledge of our *future* and final salvation (1 Thess. 5:8). However, in Ephesians, the primary focus is on the salvation that has *already* been accomplished on our behalf. In 2:1–10, in particular, we see a number of glorious truths concerning our salvation: how we have been saved *from* spiritual death, slavery and the wrath of God; how we have been saved *by* the love, mercy, grace and kindness of God in Christ; how we have been saved *through* Christ and through our being made alive in Him, and how we have been saved *for* good works that God has prepared in advance for us to do. One of the main reasons that Paul goes to such lengths to describe the wonder of our salvation is that the knowledge of this, and the continual reminder of this, act as a protective 'helmet' against all forms of spiritual discouragement.

From the helmet of salvation, Paul moves on to talk about the importance of us taking up 'the sword of the Spirit, which is the word of God'. The Roman sword was a short sword used for close combat. Here it is described as the sword 'of the Spirit', which means that it is the sword that the Spirit wields. The sword itself is the 'word of God'. There are two primary Greek words used for 'word' in the New Testament: one is the *logos*, the other is *rhema*, which is used here in 6:17. Although they are often used interchangeably, the word *rhema* tends to focus on the word that is spoken or a proclaimed word (as in 5:26), and can refer to both our defensive and offensive warfare. An example of this can be seen as Jesus in the wilderness used the sword of the Spirit, by speaking out Scripture to defend Himself against the temptations of the devil (see Matt. 4:4). However, in the context of Ephesians 6, with its reference to the gospel and the importance of its proclamation (see 6:15,19–20), it seems as if Paul would also have in mind the use of the sword as a 'weapon' to advance the cause of Christ.

Either way, it's important that we utilise this vital spiritual weapon, and realise that the sword is God's Word that we speak by the Spirit. A personal example comes to mind. When we were involved in launching KingsGate Cambridge, we had identified a great city centre venue to rent for our Sunday services. We were in advanced negotiations when suddenly we faced opposition. I remember being bombarded with fear and doubt concerning the future outcome. Then one day I was in my daily devotions and I 'happened' to come across the following promise: 'These are the words of him who is holy and true, who holds the key of David. What he opens no one can shut, and what he shuts no one can open … See, I have placed before you an open door that no one can shut' (Rev. 3:7–8). Immediately I sensed the Lord speaking a *rhema* word to me, which dispelled the doubt and fear. I took that word about 'an open door' and spoke it out in prayer. That was on a Friday. By the Monday everything had turned around and we walked through that open door!

REFLECT AND RESPOND

- **Take time to remind yourself of the wonder of your salvation in Christ by reading Ephesians 2:1–10. If you have a copy of *Transformed Life*, why not reread Week 4, which expounds these glorious verses in more detail.**

- **Make a decision to take up the sword of the Spirit, speaking out God's Word in your defence, as well as bringing His truth to others.**

- **Say this prayer: 'I place the helmet of salvation on my head. Thank You, Father, that You have saved me and all the riches of heaven are mine in Christ. I take up the sword of the Spirit. Bring Your Word to my mind as I need it, for the glory of Your name. Amen!'**

MEMORY VERSE

'Finally, be strong in the Lord and in his mighty power. Put on the full armour of God, so that you can take your stand against the devil's schemes.'

EPHESIANS 6:10–11

DEVELOP A LIFESTYLE OF PRAYER

'And pray in the Spirit on all occasions with all kinds of prayers and requests. With this in mind, be alert and always keep on praying for all the Lord's people.' **EPHESIANS 6:18**

A while ago I had the privilege of going to a gathering of leaders of key Christian denominations and streams. One of the speakers was Pastor Agu, who heads up the Redeemed Church in the UK, a huge and fast-growing church that started in Nigeria. He was talking about the importance of prayer. He said words to this effect: 'In Africa we pray about everything. We are used to praying at night that there will be water in the tap in the morning. If you are in Congo, you pray that you will safely get to your destination. Now we are in Europe we don't need to pray for these basic things, so we have more time to pray for revival.' The African Christians can teach us a lot about prayer as a lifestyle!

Developing a lifestyle of prayer is at the heart of Paul's conclusion of his all-important teaching on spiritual warfare. Whether prayer is 'the final expression of Christian weaponry in the conflict against the "powers"'[1] or more likely 'foundational for the deployment of all the other weapons',[2] the fact that we have three verses on prayer (6:18–20) emphasises the centrality of prayer in the fight against evil. This is underscored by the fourfold repetition of the word 'all', obscured in the NIV, but clearer in the ESV: 'praying at *all* times in the Spirit, with *all* prayer and supplication. To that end keep alert with *all* perseverance, making supplication for *all* the saints' (6:18, my emphasis).

Undergirding these four emphases is the call to pray 'in the Spirit', highlighting that we need the Spirit's help in this all-important matter of prayer. So the question is: how does the Spirit help us? Gordon Fee argues that when placed alongside other references like 1 Corinthians 14:14–15 and Romans 8:26–27, praying in the Spirit 'is a form of prayer in which the Spirit assumes a special role in the praying, especially, though probably not exclusively, praying in tongues'.[3] While this reference almost certainly includes the wonderful gifts of speaking in tongues, we should not limit it to this, since the Spirit helps us as we pray all different kinds of prayers.

First, with the Spirit's help we are called to pray 'on *all* occasions'. This doesn't literally mean 'all the time' but 'in every situation', as with the example used above from Pastor Agu.

Second, we are to pray 'with all kinds of prayers and requests'. There is so much about prayer in the Bible and so many different ways we can pray. As a foundation, we can pray the Lord's Prayer, not just as a set prayer but as a wonderful prayer outline. Then we can pray some of the prayers that Paul modelled for us, such as those outlined in Ephesians 1 and 3 (see *Transformed Life* weeks 3 and 7). There are many other great Bible prayers such as the 'Prayer of Jabez' (1 Chron. 4:9–10).

Third, we are to 'keep alert with *all* perseverance' (ESV, my emphasis). This call to constant alertness is a clear reminder that we are to be like watchmen, staying vigilant and determined in prayer, knowing that we are in a real wrestle with the spiritual forces of evil. In the words of one commentator: 'believers are to persevere so as to overcome fatigue and discouragement, and not to fall into spiritual sleep or complacency'.[4]

Fourth, we are to be alert and persevere in prayer 'for *all* the Lord's people' (6:18, my emphasis), that is with 'those whom [we] have been joined in the new community of God's people'.[5] This is a vital call for believers to stand together as they resist the attacks of the evil one and advance the kingdom of God. I remember many years ago using the picture of the Roman testudo to teach about the importance of every believer lifting up a 'prayer shield' over each other (see also Day 47 on the 'shield of faith'): for every member to pray for others in their small groups, for their group leaders, for their pastoral overseers and for us as senior leaders; then, similarly, for all the leaders to pray for everyone in their sphere. I would encourage all local churches to do the same, and then to pray for *other* churches and church leaders across their community and nation.

All of this highlights the importance of developing a lifestyle of prayer: praying on all occasions, with all kinds of prayers, with all perseverance, for all God's people.

REFLECT AND RESPOND

- **Consider how you can grow in developing prayer as a lifestyle. What would it mean for you to begin to pray on all occasions, with all types of prayer and with perseverance?**

- **Start praying for people in your small group and the leadership of your church on a regular basis, lifting up the 'prayer shield' over them.**

- **Pray for leaders and for the advance of the gospel.**

MEMORY VERSE

'Finally, be strong in the Lord and in his mighty power. Put on the full armour of God, so that you can take your stand against the devil's schemes.'

EPHESIANS 6:10–11

PRAY FOR LEADERS AND FOR THE ADVANCE OF THE GOSPEL

'Pray also for me, that whenever I speak, words may be given me so that I will fearlessly make known the mystery of the gospel, for which I am an ambassador in chains. Pray that I may declare it fearlessly, as I should.' **EPHESIANS 6:19–20**

Charles Spurgeon (1834–1892) is known as the 'prince of preachers'. He was a Baptist minister in England who saw enormous blessings from God upon his ministry. But Spurgeon never took credit for the success of his ministry. Instead, he always pointed to the hundreds of people who came before services and prayed for God's blessing. He said any success he had came from God in answer to their prayers. Spurgeon was often fond of calling these prayer gatherings the church's 'boiler room'. In Spurgeon's time, steam was the power source of the day. Boiler rooms were the powerhouses, the driving forces of everything from vast machines in factories to household heating systems. Boiler rooms, however, were not pleasant places to visit. They were functional, dirty, and hot; often tucked away in the basement. Likewise, Spurgeon saw the prayers of his people as the spiritual power behind his preaching and ministry. This is why he told his fellow pastors, 'Brethren, we shall never see much change for the better in our churches in general till the prayer meeting occupies a higher place in the esteem of Christians'.[1]

Spurgeon's strong focus on prayer reflects that of Paul's here in Ephesians. The apostle has already shown how he prays for the church (1:15–18; 3:14–19) and has gone on to encourage the believers to pray for each other (6:18). Here in 6:19–20 he concludes with a remarkable call for the church to pray for him. There's much that we can learn from this.

First, spiritual leaders need prayer, too! Hence we have the mighty apostle Paul twice asking for the prayer support of the Christians in the church in Ephesus: 'Pray also for me … Pray'. For almost the whole of my ministry life, I have been very much aware of the need for the prayer support of both specific individuals and of a 'Prayer Army' who have committed to pray for myself, my wife, our family and for our church as a whole. Countless are the times when I was battling with a particular issue or decision, when I suddenly felt a new freedom, peace, clarity and wisdom come. I am sure that on many of those occasions it has been because of the faithful prayers of God's people.

Second, there is a particular need to pray for those who are involved in the proclamation of the gospel. Here Paul is asking for two things: utterance and boldness. One author on prayer has written: 'air is not more necessary to lungs than prayer to the preacher … the preacher must pray, but *the preacher must be prayed for*'.[2] I would heartily concur. One of the reasons why we have groups from our Prayer Army praying on rotation both before and during our Sunday services is to pray for the preachers to be anointed and for the congregation to be receptive to the ministry of the Word.

Third, we must all imitate Paul's commitment to sharing the good news. Here Paul is in prison, and yet his number one prayer is not so much for his own needs, but that he might continue to be a faithful 'ambassador' in proclaiming the good news. It's a fitting end to this section on spiritual warfare and highlights that while we are not all called to preach like Paul, we are called to maintain a state of readiness (see Day 46) as 'witnesses'. We are those who are now children of the light and therefore Christ's ambassadors, with the huge privilege of giving opportunity for others to come into the light and be saved!

REFLECT AND RESPOND

- At the conclusion of this week, put on the full armour of God. Appropriate what is already yours in Christ by saying this prayer: 'I put on the belt of truth around my waist. Help me, Lord, to listen to and act on your truth alone and not be deceived by the devil's lies. I put on the breastplate of righteousness. Thank You that because of Your redemption, I am righteous in Christ. Help me live my life in a way that honours You. I put on the shoes of the gospel of peace. Lord, I am willing to go anywhere You ask or do anything You ask of me. I stand behind the shield of faith, secure in the knowledge of Your goodness, love and power. I place the helmet of salvation on my head. Thank You, Father, that You have saved me and all the riches of heaven are mine in Christ. I take up the sword of the Spirit. Bring Your Word to my mind as I need it, for the glory of Your name. Amen.'

- Take some extra time to pray in the Spirit for other believers and spiritual leaders, especially for those involved in the proclamation of the gospel.

- Ask the Lord to empower You and help You to share the good news in word and deed.

MEMORY VERSE

'Finally, be strong in the Lord and in his mighty power. Put on the full armour of God, so that you can take your stand against the devil's schemes.'

EPHESIANS 6:10–11

CONCLUSION

'Tychicus, the dear brother and faithful servant in the Lord, will tell you everything, so that you also may know how I am and what I am doing. I am sending him to you for this very purpose, that you may know how we are, and that he may encourage you. Peace to the brothers and sisters, and love with faith from God the Father and the Lord Jesus Christ. Grace to all who love our Lord Jesus Christ with an undying love'
EPHESIANS 6:21–24

If I was to look back at my thirty-plus years as a Christian, I am so grateful for kingdom relationships. First, I'm immensely thankful for the glorious privilege of coming to know an eternal Father God, who in Christ and through His Spirit has saved me, filled me and is still completely transforming my whole life. Second, I'm so appreciative of being in His family, the Church. Over the years, Karen and I have been blessed with many wonderful brothers and sisters in Christ, who are also faithful co-workers, both within KingsGate and in the wider body of Christ in this nation and overseas.

Throughout Ephesians Paul has highlighted the centrality of these vertical and horizontal relationships, and has given multiple encouragements as to how we are to invest in the development of these. Here in 6:21–24 he models something for us, both in his references to his fellow worker, Tychicus, through his concern for the wellbeing of the Church, and through his benediction for them in the name of the Father and the Son.

First, it's worth noting Paul's mention of Tychicus. Unlike some 'strong' leaders, Paul didn't champion independence as a virtue, but rather throughout his life and ministry highlighted the importance of being part of a loving and supportive team. Here, he refers very warmly to Tychicus, one of his team members (see Acts 20:4), as 'the dear brother and faithful servant in the Lord'.

Paul not only demonstrates his love for his ministry colleague, but also his love and concern for the church in Ephesus. The fact that he has written this letter from prison shows how much he cares for these Ephesian Christians. He is sending Tychicus as the likely bringer of the letter (and probably the letter to the Colossians, too), and as the bearer of news concerning Paul himself. Three times Paul states that the Ephesian church would receive an update concerning how he himself was doing. Although the personal greetings that we find in Colossians chapter 4 are largely absent here, Paul is nevertheless keen to update the Ephesians with his personal news. His purpose in doing this was for their benefit: so that they might be encouraged.

Having demonstrated his love and concern for his readers, Paul now concludes his letter with a twofold prayer or benediction (an invocation for God to bring blessing). In the first benediction Paul asks for the Father and the Son to bestow peace, love, and faith upon these believers. This emphasis on peace is in accord with the importance of this concept throughout the letter. Peace comes from God through Christ, but is also something 'that unites all believers into one body'.[1] Here Paul is praying for an ongoing and deeper experience of this peace. Similarly he prays that the church might experience a deeper dimension of the Father's love, a major focus of the letter and a primary emphasis of his prayer in 3:14–19. Then he prays that they might grow and be strengthened in their faith.

In his second benediction, Paul moves from 'peace' to 'grace', and in so doing returns to the theme of his opening greeting in 1:1–2. Like peace, grace was central to Paul's whole theology, both throughout his letters and specifically here in Ephesians. This 'grace' is the unmerited favour of God, and is essential for salvation (2:4–10), for our ongoing life as Christians (1:1–2) and for our ministry as Christians (3:1–13; 4:8). Hence, Paul's prayer for more grace!

However, rather than say simply, 'Grace to all of you,' he says, 'grace to all who love our Lord Jesus Christ.' This is not saying that His grace is conditional upon our love. But he is highlighting that to be truly in Christ (and a recipient of His grace) will result in a real personal relationship with Christ, and will rebound in love for Him. The term 'undying love' has been variously interpreted either as our eternal love for Jesus, or as linked to God and His grace. If it's the latter then Paul is praying that God will bless His people not only with grace, but also with an experience of eternal life in the here and now. A fitting end to this wonderful letter to the Ephesians!

REFLECT AND RESPOND

- **Take time to thank God for the relationships that you have within the body of Christ. Consider at the close of this study how you can grow in demonstrating the love of God to those in the Church, your family and your 'world'.**

- **Take these two benedictions and apply them to your own life and those of others in your group and church: 'Peace to you and love with faith from God the Father and the Lord Jesus Christ. Grace to you who love our Lord Jesus Christ with an undying love.'**

ENDNOTES

Introduction

[1] J.A. Robinson, *St Paul's Epistle to the Ephesians* (Macmillan, 1994), vii.

[2] R.E. Brown, *An Introduction to the New Testament* (Doubleday, 1997), p620. Both Robinson and Brown found cited in P.T. O'Brien, *The Letter to the Ephesians* (Cambridge: Eerdmans, 1999), p1.

[3] J.R.W. Stott, *The Message of Ephesians: God's New Society* (Leicester, Inter-Varsity Press, 1979), p146.

[4] *Reveal* survey by Willow Creek. See for example Greg Hawkins and Cally Parkinson, *Follow Me* (Willow Creek Association, 2008), p41.

Day 1

[1] Victor Hugo, *Les Miserables* (Penguin Classics; Reprint edition, 1982). Originally published in 1862. Public domain.

Day 2

[1] www.bbc.co.uk/archive/princesselizabeth/ (accessed June 2016).

Day 3

[1] Jim Collins, *Good to Great* (London: Collins Business, 2001).

[2] Jim Collins, *How the Mighty Fall* (Random House Business, 2009).
[3] C.S. Lewis, *Mere Christianity* (C.S. Lewis Pte Ltd, 1942, 1943, 1944, 1952). Used by permission.

Day 4

[1] Markus Barth, cited in Stott (ibid.), pp153–154.

[2] Rick Warren, *The Purpose Driven Life* (Grand Rapids: Zondervan, 2012), pp160–167.

Day 5

[1] A.T. Lincoln, 'Ephesians', *Word Biblical Commentary*, Vol 42 (Thomas Nelson, 1990).

Day 6

[1] Terry Virgo, *Does the Future Have a Church?* (Kingsway, 2003), p96.

Day 7

[1] O'Brien, ibid.
[2] C.H. Spurgeon, *Commentary on Ephesians* (Titus Books, 2014).

Day 9

[1] Story recounted by Tom Webster at KingsGate Community Church. Own paraphrasing.

[2] Robert Madu, heard preaching at the HTB (Holy Trinity Brompton) Leadership Conference, May 2015, at the Royal Albert Hall, London.

Day 10

[1] B. Hybels, *Courageous Leadership* (Zondervan, 2002), p27.

[2] C.E. Arnold, *Ephesians: Exegetical Commentary on the New Testament* (Grand Rapids: Zondervan, 2010), p256.

[3] C.E. Arnold, ibid, p259.

[4] C.E. Arnold, ibid, p261.

Day 12

[1] Steven Covey, *The Seven Habits of Highly Effective People* (New York: Free Press, 2004), p98.

[2] John Piper, *Desiring God* (Multnomah, 1994), p19.

[3] Klyne Snodgrass, *The NIV Application Commentary: Ephesians* (Grand Rapids: Zondervan, 1996).

[4] Martyn Lloyd-Jones, *Christian Unity: An Exposition of Ephesians 4:1–16* (Baker Books, 1998), pp210–11.

Day 13

[1] Terry Virgo, ibid, p126.

Day 15

[1] Martyn Lloyd-Jones, *Darkness and Light: An Exposition of Ephesians 4:17–5:17* (Edinburgh: Banner of Truth, 1982), p37.

Day 16

[1] J.W.R. Stott, *The Message of Ephesians* (Leicester: Inter-Varsity, 1979), p180.

[2] Charles Hodge, *Ephesians* (Wheaton, Illinois: Crossway, 1994) p158.

Day 17

[1] Martyn Lloyd-Jones, *Darkness and Light: An Exposition of Ephesians 4:17–5:17* (Edinburgh: Banner of Truth, 1982) p219.

Day 21

[1] Summary based on 'From Wounded to Whole: Making Room for Forgiveness' in Bill Hybels, *Simplify: Ten Practices to Unclutter your Soul* (Hodder and Stoughton, 2014).

Day 22

[1] *Our Daily Bread II* (Thomas Nelson, 2005) p330.

Day 23

[1] J.W.R. Stott. ibid, p192.

[2] P.T. O'Brien, ibid, pp323, 359.

[3] A.T. Lincoln, ibid, p322.

[4] C.E. Arnold, ibid, p320.

Day 24

[1] John Cleese, *So, Anyway…: The Autobiography* (Arrow, 2015).

[2] Arnold, ibid, quoting P.W. van der Horst, 'Is Wittiness Un-Christian?', *Miscellanea Neotestamentica*.

[3] O'Brien, ibid, citing J.L. Houlden's, *Paul's Letters from Prison: Philippians, Colossians, Philemon and Ephesians* (Philadelphia: Westminster Press, 1977), p324.

[4] Martyn Lloyd-Jones, *Darkness and Light* (ibid), p335–36.

Day 25

[1] O'Brien, ibid, p363.

[2] O'Brien, ibid, p364.

[3] O'Brien, ibid, p365.

Day 27

[1] Martyn Lloyd-Jones, *Darkness and Light* (ibid), pp420–22.

[2] Charles G. Finney, *Experiencing Revival* (Whitaker House, 2000).

Day 28

[1] From J. Gillies, *Memoirs of the Life of the Reverend George Whitefield MA*, cited by A.A. Dallimore, *George Whitefield: The Life and Times of the Great Evangelist of the Eighteenth-Century Revival*, Vol. 1 (Banner of Truth, 1970), pp263–64.

Day 29

[1] Martyn Lloyd-Jones, *Darkness and Light* (ibid), p426.

Day 30

[1] O'Brien, ibid, p382.

[2] O'Brien, ibid, p383.

Day 31

[1] Arnold, ibid.

Day 32

[1] H.A.W. Meyer, *Critical and Exegetical Handbook to the Epistle to the Ephesians and the Epistle to Philemon* (Edin, 1880), p285, op cit Fee, *God's Empowering Presence*, p721, footnote 195.

Day 33

[1] Arnold, ibid, p352.

[2] G. Fee, *God's Empowering Presence* (Hendrickson, 1994), p653.

[3] O'Brien, ibid, p395.

Day 34

[1] Corrie Ten Boom, *The Hiding Place* (Hodder & Stoughton, 2004)

[2] O'Brien, ibid, p396.

Day 35

[1] Martin Lloyd-Jones, *Life in the Spirit: In Marriage, Home and Work: An Exposition of Ephesians 5:18–6:9* (Banner of Truth, 1982), p74.

Day 36

[1] Arnold, ibid, p364.

Day 37

[1] J.W. Hayford, *Spirit-Filled Life New Testament Commentary Series: Ephesians & Colossians* (Nashville: Thomas Nelson, 2005), pp111–12.

[2] Stott, ibid, p229.

[3] Hayford, ibid, p113.

Day 38

[1] Stott, ibid, p230.

Day 39

[1] Hayford, ibid, p114.

[2] Arnold, ibid, p417.

Day 40

[1] Arnold, ibid, p417.

[2] O'Brien, ibid, p447.

[3] Stott, ibid, p245.

[4] Stott, ibid, p246.

[5] John Calvin translation cited by Stott (ibid), p247.

Day 41

[1] Stott, p259.

[2] Summarised from Arnold (ibid).

Day 42

[1] Stott, ibid, p254.

[2] Stott, ibid, p254.

Day 44

[1] Story based on information from *Our Daily Bread*, 3 May 1994, available at odb.org/1994/05/03/standing-firm/

[2] C.S. Lewis, *The Screwtape Letters* (copyright C.S. Lewis Pte Ltd, 1942). Used by permission.

Day 45

[1] Arnold, ibid.

[2] G.G. Findlay, cited by Stott (ibid), p279.

Day 46

[1] Brian McCoic, www.mcclatchydc.com/latest-news/article24436039.html

[2] O'Brien, ibid, p480.

Day 48

[1] Fee, ibid, p730.

[2] Arnold, ibid.

[3] Fee, ibid, pp730–31.

[4] O'Brien, ibid, p485.

[5] O'Brien, pp485–86.

Day 49

[1] C.H. Spurgeon, *Only a Prayer Meeting* (Christian Focus Publications, 2010).

[2] E.M. Bounds, *The Complete Works of E.M. Bounds on Prayer* (Baker Books, 1990).

Day 50

[1] Arnold, ibid.

TRANSFORMED (LIFE)

Grow together as your whole church explores true identity, belonging and purpose through Ephesians 1–3. This seven-week church programme is ideal as a stand-alone programme or as the first part of a series with *Transformed Living*.

Transformed Life resources include:
• Free sermon outlines
• Free small group videos and studies
• Free online youth resources
• *Transformed Life*, a 50-day devotional
• Activity books for early and primary years

For more information about the resources, bulk discounts and to sign up, visit **www.transformed-life.info**

SmallGroup central

All of our small group ideas and resources in one place

Online:

www.smallgroupcentral.org.uk
is filled with free video teaching, tools, articles and a whole host of ideas.

On the road:

A range of seminars themed for small groups can be brought to your local community. Contact us at ***hello@smallgroupcentral.org.uk***

In print:

Books, study guides and DVDs covering an extensive list of themes, Bible books and life issues.

Log on and find out more at:
www.smallgroupcentral.org.uk

Courses and seminars

Waverley Abbey College

Publishing and media

Conference facilities

Transforming lives

CWR's vision is to enable people to experience personal transformation through applying God's Word to their lives and relationships.

Our Bible-based training and resources help people around the world to:
• Grow in their walk with God
• Understand and apply Scripture to their lives
• Resource themselves and their church
• Develop pastoral care and counselling skills
• Train for leadership
• Strengthen relationships, marriage and family life and much more.

Our insightful writers provide daily Bible reading notes and other resources for all ages, and our experienced course designers and presenters have gained an international reputation for excellence and effectiveness.

CWR's Training and Conference Centres in Surrey, England, provides excellent facilities in idyllic settings – ideal for both learning and spiritual refreshment.

CWR Applying God's Word to everyday life and relationships

CWR, Waverley Abbey House,
Waverley Lane, Farnham,
Surrey GU9 8EP, UK

Telephone: **+44 (0)1252 784700**
Email: **info@cwr.org.uk**
Website: **www.cwr.org.uk**

Registered Charity No. 294387
Company Registration No. 1990308